The Basics Of Christianity

JOSHUA FOGLE

DEDICATION

I dedicate this book to God, there is no other.

CONTENTS

FOREWORD

What are The Basics of Christianity? What is it that we should actually know about the fundamental foundations stones of The Christian Faith? Have you ever stopped to consider this of yourself? In this book, if it be the will of God, this will be what we will discover together as we journey through The Holy Scriptures and some of the historical writings of early Christianity. We shall see from Holy Writ exactly how the death of Christ Jesus our Lord upon The Cross reconciles us to God, and how His blood redeems us, sanctifies us, and justifies us to God through His blood washing away our sins. We shall see the three ways we are born again according to Holy Writ, and that we are made a new creature through Christ Jesus our Lord for we are made a child of God through faith in Him. We shall also discover the historical declarations for The Books of The Bible, as well as see the evidence for Christianity that God declared would cause belief in Him. We shall also learn that The Holy Bible reveals that it alone is the standard of Christian doctrine, and that early Christianity sought to its pages alone to learn the will and mind of God. We shall also see that there are three major points that we are able to discover through Scripture that reveal unto us a true Christian lifestyle, and we shall also see some of the fulfilled Biblical signs that we are living in the end times. This and more by the leading and blessing of God we shall discover together within this book, if God permit. Amen.

WHAT IS CHRISTIANITY?

What are the basics of Christianity? What do Christians believe? What is it that Christian know, that others do not know? What don't I know? What should I know as a Christian? Have you ever thought any of these questions to yourself? Have you ever asked: Who is God? Is God real? What happens to us when we die? As a believer myself, I am sure that there are many Christians and none Christians who haven't the slightest idea what it is that Christianity is all about even it they think they do. For Christianity in the popular media, the mega-churches, political Christianity, liberal Christianity, and conspiracy theory Christianity is far different then what The Bible actually teaches and says. Now rather then having an expose on these things, we are instead going to discuss using The Bible and historical documentation, exactly what Christianity is and is not, for we will see that both The Bible and early Christianity declare that The Holy Bible alone is Christian doctrine in entirety, and incorporated with that, we will see the historical attestation for The Biblical Canon, that is, The Books of The Bible, and a discussion on Bible Versions. Then we will move on to what The Bible actually teaches on how salvation from sin Biblically works, how a Christian is to Biblically live their life, what happens when we die and the hereafter, The Holy Trinity, and the importance and necessity of keeping The Law of God and The Seventh-day Sabbath of God, and what it truly means when Scripture says to not judge others, as well as how faith and works combine in Holy Writ.

Now before we truly begin in earnest, let us start with that which really is the basics of what most people know in the western world concerning Christianity, by reading two of the most popular quotation passages from Scripture. We read: "For God so loved the world, that he gave his only begotten Son, that whosoever believeth in him should not perish, but have everlasting life. For God sent not his Son into the world to condemn the world; but that the world through him might be saved. He that believeth on him is not condemned: but he that believeth not is condemned already, because he hath not believed in the name of the only begotten Son of God. (John 3:16-18) But he was wounded for our transgressions, he was bruised for our iniquities: the chastisement of our peace was upon him; and with his stripes we are healed. (Isaiah 53:5). And with this as our basic and foundation, let us begin.

Chapter One: What Is Christianity?

Our introduction to what we will be discussing in this book.

Chapter Two: The Bible And Its Books

In this chapter we discuss The Biblical necessity of reading Holy Writ, and the historical attestation for The Books of The Bible, as well as on the importance of The Bible Version debate.

Chapter Three: How And Why Humanity Is Sinful

It has been asked: Why did God allow sin and why is there so much suffering in the world? And as we shall Biblically see, God allows us all freedom of choice, and because of the free choice of Adam and Eve we all receive their propensity to sin even though we do not receive their actually sin as we discuss in this chapter specifically.

Chapter Four: How God Removes Our Sins Through Jesus Christ

This chapter is the heart of this book, just as this topic is the heart of Christianity, for as we shall see and learn through Holy Writ, we discover that we are all separated from God because of our sins, which means God will not even hear us, therefore God reconciles us to Himself through the death of Christ, so that we can die through Christ through Baptism and thus be reconciled unto God, for the penalty of sin which is death has been fulfilled. We shall also discuss some of the other points that Scripture reveals unto us concerning how we are saved through Christ Jesus our Lord, and the three methods that Scripture reveals unto us in how we are Born Again.

Chapter Five: What It Means To Live A Christian Life

Belief in Christ Jesus our Lord without walking the path of Christ in this life, is to have nothing more then the exact same belief system of the Devil who also knows exactly who Christ is and that Christ is God. Therefore in this chapter, we discuss the three duties that every Christian has in order to actually be a real Christian as Scripture reveals.

Chapter Six: Understanding The Holy Trinity

The Holy Trinity is perhaps the most misunderstood doctrine in Christianity, if not the most challenged doctrine, yet in this chapter specifically, we shall discover together, that Holy Writ makes it abundantly clear that our One and Only God is Jehovah, and that no one has The Name Jehovah except Jehovah, and that God The Father, God The Son, and God The Most Holy Ghost are all The One Jehovah, even though they are all three separate and distinct individuals at the same time as Scripture reveals.

Chapter Seven: Bible Prophecy And Christianity

Bible prophecy is perhaps the most thrilling aspect of learning imaginable, for it both sets Christianity beyond the skeptics reach, and gives one reason to believe as our Lord and Savior Jesus Christ reveals. Therefore, in this chapter we are going to discover the prophetic declaration of when The Messiah, our Lord Jesus Christ was to arrive at His first coming, that was written down before it happened and happened exactly as it was written to the exact year period as it was revealed through the pages of Holy Writ in Daniel chapter nine.

Chapter Eight: What Really Happens When We Die According To The Bible?

There is to much misconception concerning what happens when we die that Christians have accepted without full investigation from what Holy Writ reveals, for as we shall see, Holy Scripture makes it very clear that when we die we have not mental thinking power or thoughts upon death, for man neither has an immortal soul or spirit as the common understanding of these things are, for only God has immortality as The Bible reveals, and as we shall also see revealed through Holy Writ, the wicked who face the punishment of the fires of Hell do not suffer torment for all eternity as some suppose, but rather face eternal death were they are consumed by the fire and are forever in the oblivion and unthinking state of death, for only the righteous receive eternal life and abide forever as Holy Writ reveals.

Chapter Nine: The Law Of God And The Seventh-Day Sabbath

In this chapter, we see the ever necessity and perpetual nature of The Ten Commandments that we as Christians are required to keep as Holy Writ commands, and this includes the necessity of keeping The Seventh-day Sabbath of God as revealed in the fourth commandment. This and a discussion on how faith and works combine in Holy Writ, as well as the true meaning of not judging others so that we are not judged is discussed in this chapter specifically.

Chapter Ten: Evidence For Christianity

In this chapter we see one of the greatest evidences for Christianity, for as we shall see, Holy Writ reveals unto us before it happened, the declaration that there would be four kingdoms upon this world that would supersede each other starting with Babylon, and that the territory of the fourth kingdom that was never part of the three other kingdoms would brake apart into ten kingdoms, and this has indeed happened exactly as Scripture declared that it would, which was written down and declared before it happened, and this using the skeptics dates for The Book of Daniel.

Chapter Eleven: The Second Coming Of Christ According To Scripture

We see from Holy Writ, that that our Lord and Savior Jesus Christ hath declared that He would come again to take us to Himself unto Heavenly Jerusalem and The Kingdom of God, both those whom He will resurrect from the dead, and those alive at His Second Coming, and this as we shall see from Holy Writ is truly near at the door as Scripture reveals unto us, for as we shall see in this chapter, there are signs of the nearness of The Second Coming of Christ that have been fulfilled, of which we shall discuss some of these declared signs in this chapter specifically.

Chapter Twelve: Conclusion

Closing remarks and a final thought.

Chapter Thirteen: Necessary Reading

The only Book that is truly necessary reading is The Book, The Holy Bible, and it is to Its Sacred Pages that we must resort into totally for all things pertaining to the things of God, for only The Bible is infallible and true with all other things potentially containing error if not deliberate deception, that said, the books in this chapter have been my personal delight to use for research, therefore, considering many of them are old titles, lest they be lost to the oblivion of time, and because it seems important to me, they are here presented and preserved as long as this book may last. Amen.

THE BIBLE AND ITS BOOKS

All scripture is given by inspiration of God, and is profitable for doctrine, for reproof, for correction, for instruction in righteousness: That the man of God may be perfect, thoroughly furnished unto all good works. (2 Timothy 3:16-17) For whatsoever things were written aforetime were written for our learning, that we through patience and comfort of the scriptures might have hope. (Romans 15:4) With this, we come to the ever important and necessary topic of every Christians duty and privilege of Reading Holy Scripture for themselves, for as we shall see in this chapter specifically, it is through The Bible, and The Bible Alone that we learn the will of God for our lives, so that we will be made fit for The Kingdom of Heaven, and are then able to enter in through the gates of New Jerusalem were God dwells.

The Importance Of Reading The Bible

For this is good and acceptable in the sight of God our Saviour; Who will have all men to be saved, and to come unto the knowledge of the truth. (1 Timothy 2:3-4) And what is The Truth? The Holy Bible as we read: "Sanctify them through thy truth: thy word is truth. (John 17:17). Now consider what our Lord and Savior Jesus Christ declares for He saith: "Then Jesus said unto them, Verily, verily, I say unto you, Except ye eat the flesh of the Son of man, and drink his blood, ye have no life in you. (John 6:53-54) And what doth out Lord Jesus Christ mean when He says we must eat His flesh to receive eternal life? It means, as He clarifies, to take His Words unto ourselves as we read: "It is the spirit that quickeneth; the flesh profiteth nothing: the words that I speak unto you, they are spirit, and they are life. (John 6:63) Therefore we must "take the helmet of salvation, and the sword of the Spirit, which is the word of God: (Ephesians 6:17)

Therefore "Seek ye out of the book of the LORD, and read: (Isaiah 34:16) As newborn babes, desire the sincere milk of the word, that ye may grow thereby: (1 Peter 2:2) For "It is written, Man shall not live by bread alone, but by every word that proceedeth out of the mouth of God. (Matthew 4:4). For saith our Lord Jesus Christ: "Verily, verily, I say unto you, He that heareth my word, and believeth on him that sent me, hath everlasting life, and shall not come into condemnation; but is passed from death unto life. (John 5:24).

And now, whom did God deliver His Words unto that we might receive it of their hand and thus believe? We learn that through the Apostles of our Lord Jesus Christ that we receive The Word of God. We read: "But the Comforter, which is the Holy Ghost, whom the Father will send in my name, he shall teach you all things, and bring all things to your remembrance, whatsoever I have said unto you. (John 14:26) Howbeit when he, the Spirit of truth, is come, he will guide you into all truth: for he shall not speak of himself; but whatsoever he shall hear, that shall he speak: and he will shew you things to come. (John 16:13) But when the Comforter is come, whom I will send unto you from the Father, even the Spirit of truth, which proceedeth from the Father, he shall testify of me: (John 15:26)

Which things also we speak, not in the words which men's wisdom teacheth, but which the Holy Ghost teacheth; comparing spiritual things with spiritual. (1 Corinthians 2:13) And take the helmet of salvation, and the sword of the Spirit, which is the word of God: (Ephesians 6:17) For this cause also thank we God without ceasing, because, when ye received the word of God which ye heard of us, ye received it not as the word of men, but as it is in truth, the word of God, which effectually worketh also in you that believe. (1 Thessalonians 2:13) For we write none other things unto you, that what ye read or acknowledge; and I trust ye shall acknowledge even to the end; (2 Corinthians 1:13) If any man teach otherwise, and consent not to the wholesome words, even the words of our Lord Jesus Christ, and to the doctrine which is according to godliness; He is proud, knowing nothing, (1 Timothy 6:3-4) These things have I written unto you that believe on the name of the Son of God; that ye may know that ye have eternal life, and that ye may believe on the name of the Son of God. (1 John 5:13) We are of God: he that knoweth God heareth us; he that is not of God heareth not us. Hereby know we the spirit of truth, and the spirit of error. (1 John 4:6)

Therefore, seeing as the apostle has written unto us (See 1 John 5:13; Consider 2 Timothy 3:16-17; Romans 15:4), for The New Testament was written in their day (Consider and Compare 1 Timothy 5:18; Deuteronomy 25:4; Luke 10:7; See 2 Peter 3:15-16), let us fulfilled The Biblical command to "take the helmet of salvation, and the sword of the Spirit, which is the word of God: (Ephesians 6:17) unto ourselves, for in this way we will learn The Will of God for our lives, and receive belief in Him and thus be saved from all iniquity, for "He that believeth and is baptized shall be saved; but he that believeth not shall be damned. (Mark 16:16 Compare Matthew 7:21; John 14:24; also John 8:47; Jeremiah 36:6-8; 2 Corinthians 1:13). Amen.

The History Of The Biblical Canon

History reveals that which the enemies of Christianity try to imply that it does not, that is, that we know exactly what The Books of The Bible actually are. Therefore now, let us consider the voice of antiquity, that is, the voice of early Christianity that indeed reveals and declares The Canon of The New Testament. We read from Rufinus (A.D. 344 or 345 to A.D. 410) in his work entitled: "A Commentary On The Apostles' Creed." Where he declares the following concerning The Books of The Bible:

"And therefore it seems proper in this place to enumerate, as we have learnt from the traditions of the Fathers, the books of the New and the Old Testament, which, according to the tradition of our forefathers, are believed to have been inspired by the Holy Ghost, and have been handed down to the Churches of Christ. Of the Old Testament, therefore, first of all there have been handed down five books of Moses, Genesis, Exodus, Leviticus, Numbers, Deuteronomy; Then Jesus Nave, (Joshua the son of Nun), The book of Judges together with Ruth; then four books of Kings (Reigns), which the Hebrews reckon two; the Book of Omissions, which is entitled the Book of Days (Chronicles), two books of Ezra (Ezra and Nehemiah), which the Hebrews reckon one, and Esther; of the Prophets, Isaiah, Jeremiah, Ezekiel, and Daniel ; moreover of the twelve (minor) Prophets, one book; Job also and the Psalms of David, each one book. Solomon gave three books to the Churches, Proverbs, Ecclesiastes, Canticles. These comprise the books of the Old Testament. Of the New there are four Gospels, Matthew, Mark, Luke, John; the Acts of the Apostles, written by Luke; fourteen Epistles of the Apostle Paul, two of the Apostle Peter, one of James, brother of the Lord and Apostle, one of Jude, three of John, the Revelation of John. These are the books which the Fathers have comprised within the Canon, and from which they would have us deduce the proofs of our faith. But it should be known that there are also other books which our fathers call not "Canonical" but "Ecclesiastical:" that is to say, Wisdom, called the Wisdom of Solomon, and another Wisdom, called the Wisdom of the Son of Syrach, which last-mentioned the Latins call by the general title Ecclesiasticus, designating not the author of the book, but the character of the writing. To the same class belong the Book of Tobit, and the Book of Judith, and the Books of the Maccabees. In the New Testament the little book which is called the Book of the Pastor of Hermas, [and that] which is called The Two Ways,' or the Judgments of Peter; all of which they would have read in the Churches, but not appealed to for the confirmation of doctrine. The other writings they have named "Apocrypha." These they would not have read in the Churches. These are the traditions which the Fathers have handed down to us, which, as I said, I have thought it opportune to set forth in this place, for the instruction of those who are taught the first elements of the Church and of the Faith, that they may know from what fountains of the Word of God their draughts must take." (A)

We get a list of the inspired writers of the New Testament from Origen (From A.D. 185 to A.D. 253-254) in his fourteenth (thirteenth) homily on Genesis we read: "Isaac therefore dug Wells, and the Followers of Isaac dug too, The Followers of Isaac are Matthew, Mark, Luke, John. The Followers of Isaac are Peter, James, and Jude. The Apostle Paul is a Follower of Isaac. For all these dig the Wells of the New Testament." (B)

We get a further list from the same Origen in his Commentary on Joshua (seventh homily) we read: "When our Lord Jesus Christ came in the flesh, (He whose advent Jesus the son of Nun prefigured,) He made his apostles walk as priests, bearing the trumpets of the grand and heavenly doctrine of the preached word. It was Matthew who, in his Gospel, first sounded the sacerdotal clarion. Then Mark, then Luke, then John, each in succession blew his trumpet. After them Peter burst forth with the two trumpets of his epistles, Then comes James, and then Jude. Then comes John, to send forth, in addition to his previous blast, fresh sounds of his trumpet by his epistles and Apocalypse and so also does Luke, in putting forth his Acts of the Apostles. Last comes, in his turn, he who said, (1 Cor. iv. 9,) 'I think that God hath set forth us the apostles last.' When he wakes the thunders of his trumpets by his fourteen epistles, he overturned from their very foundation the walls of Jericho,–all the war-engines of idolatry, all the tenets of false philosophy." (C)

We get a catalog of the Books of the New Testament from Anthanasius Bishop of Alexandria who received the episcopate in June 8th, A.D. 328 and gives us a complete catalog of the New Testament as we receive it in our Bibles in his "Festal Epistles" the Thirty-Ninth Letter we read thus:

"But we must not look upon it as a task to speak of the books of the *New* Testament. These then are, the four Gospels, according to Matthew, Mark, Luke, and John. Afterwards, the Acts of the Apostles, and the Catholic Epistles, called of the Apostles, seven in number, viz. of James, one; of Peter, two; of John, three; and then, one of Jude. Besides these, there are fourteen Epistles of the Apostle Paul, written in this order. The first, to the Romans; then two to the Corinthians; after these, to the Galatians; next, to the Ephesians; then to the Philippians and to the Colossians; after these, two to the Thessalonians, and then to the Hebrews; and again, two to Timothy; one to Titus; and lastly, that to Philemon. To these, the Revelation of John. These are the fountains of salvation, that he who thirsteth may be satisfied with the words' they contain. In these alone is proclaimed the doctrine of godliness. Let no man add to them, neither let him take ought from them. For on this point the Lord put to shame the Sadducees, saying, *Ye do err, not knowing the Scriptures.* And He reproved the Jews, saying, *Search the Scriptures, for they testify of Me.*" (D)

(A) Quoted From: "A Select Library Of The Nicene And Post-Nicene Fathers Of The Christian Church. Second Series. Translated Into English With Prolegomena And Explanatory Notes Under The Editorial Supervision Of Philip Schaff And Henry Wace In Connection With A Number Of Patristic Scholars Of Europe And America Volume III. Theodoret, Jerome, Gennadius, Rufinus: Historical Writings, ETC. 1892. New York: The Christian Literature Company, Oxford & London : Parker & Company."

(B) Quoted From: "The Canon Of The New Testament Vindicated; In Answer To The Objections Of J. Toland, In His Amyntor. By John Richardson 1619 London: Printed By W. Bowyer, For Richard Sare, Near Gray's-Inn-Gate In Holborn."

(C) Quoted From: The Canon Of The Holy Scriptures From The Double Point Of View Of Science And Of Faith. By L. Gaussen 1862 London: James Nisbet And Co., 21 Berners Street.

(D) Quoted From: A Library Of The Fathers Of The Holy Catholic Church, Anterior To The Division Of The East And West: Translated By The Members Of The English Church 1854 Oxford, John Henry Parker; F. And J. Rivington, London. The Festal Epistles Of S. Anthanasius, Bishop Of Alexandria, Translated From The Syriac, With Notes And Indices.

The Cannon Of The Old And New Testament Ascertained, Or, The Bible Complete Without The Apocrypha And Unwritten Traditions. By

Archibald Alexander 1851 Philadelphia: Presbyterian Board Of Publications, No. 265 Chestnut Street.

The Bible Of Every Land. A History Of The Sacred Scriptures In Every Language And Dialect Into Which Translations Have Been Made: Illustrated By Specimen Portions In Native Characters; Series Of Alphabets ; Coloured Ethnographical Maps, Tables, Indexes, ECT. New Edition, Enlarged And Enriched. London: Samuel Bagster And Sons : At The Warehouse For Bibles, New Testaments, Church Services, Prayer Books, Lexicons, Grammars, Concordances, And Psalters, In Ancient And Modern Languages ; 15, Paternoster Row. 1860.

The Bible Versions Debate Explained

Seeing as we have learned from Holy Writ our great need to ever take The Holy Bible unto ourselves and read Its Sacred Pages, and, that the controversy that the enemies of Christianity wish to lay at our feet that we do not know what The Books of The Bible actually are is totally baseless as we have seen from the voice of antiquity and history. We are left with only two final controversy concerning The Bible, and this second to the last controversy, is over the actually text of Holy Writ itself, that is, Bible Versions, for as we shall see the modern versions of The Bible are not in accordance with what The Bible declares is The True Text of Holy Scripture, because they are based upon a small number of contradictory old manuscripts of The New Testament, while The King James Version translated from the majority of ancient hand written manuscripts of The New Testament, written in the original Greek, that are called and referred to as The Textus Receptus, which are found all over ancient Christendom (Africa, Asia, Europe*), does Biblically qualify as The True Text of Holy Writ as we shall see.

Therefore now, let us ask and clarify the most pertinent question when it comes to The Bible Version debate, which is: What does The Bible itself say on this subject, for as we see, when we let Holy Writ speak for itself, it condemns these minority manuscripts that contradict each other, and points to the Majority Manuscripts, and to the Textus Receptus specifically as that which we should follow. Holy Writ declares that God is not the author of confusion (See 1 Corinthians 14:33). Therefore on the basis of this alone, we must reject these minority manuscripts that contradict each other. However, Scripture goes further. It reveals that there is safety in the multitude of counselors (See Proverbs 11:14), and that a thing is established by the multitude of counselors (See Proverbs 15:22), and seeing that The

Word of God is our counselor (Compare Psalm 119:24; Psalm 119:88-89; Matthew 4:4) we can conclude that in the majority of manuscripts that contain The Word of God, there is safety, which is another reason to reject the minority of manuscripts that contradict this vast majority.

We also see declared from early Christendom that the early Christians went about everywhere spreading Christianity and leaving copies of The Gospels (**), which shows why the majority of manuscripts of The New Testament that are found everywhere indeed contain the true text of The New Testament, which when we consider also that early Christendom reveals unto us that there were heretical groups that made copies of The Gospels that contradicted each other (***), we can see yet another reason to reject these minority manuscripts of The New Testament that contradict each other, and instead accept only The Majority Text, that is, The Textus Receptus and The King James Version which is translated from these majority manuscripts.

It should be pointed out that there are over 5,000 ancient handwritten manuscripts of The New Testament in Greek, of which the vast majority of these manuscripts generally agree (80-90%)****. Now, let us consider exactly how horrendously the minority manuscripts are at variance with each other, for it is because of these type of manuscripts, that texts of Holy Writ have been removed, or a question mark to the validity of certain passages has been placed in modern versions of The Bible, such as the passages of Mark 16:9-20, were the text has been challenged because three manuscripts omit the passage, most notably ℵ and B, of which as we shall see discussed concerning these two manuscripts, they are in utter disagreement with each other in other instances, while there are six hundred and eighteen manuscripts that are able to contain these verses of Mark 16:9-20, and do contain these verses. Of which it must be noted that Irenæus from the second to third century (A.D. 120 to A.D. 202) specifically quotes verses nineteen of Mark chapter sixteen in his work "Against Heresies" book 3 chapter 10, were he states through his writing: "Also, towards the conclusion of his Gospel Mark says: "So then, after the Lord Jesus had spoken to them, He was received up into heaven, and sitteth on the right hand of God;" (A)

And now, let us consider the utter variance that the minority text manuscripts form apart of, through the writings of one who considered this topic in great detail, and so we turn to John William Burgon Dean of Chichester in his book "The Revision Revised" were we quote from page 15-17 that states: "What we are just now insisting upon is only the *depraved text* of codices ℵ A B C D, --Especially of ℵ B D. And because this is a matter which lies at the root of the whole controversy, and because we cannot afford that there shall exist in our reader's mind the slightest doubt on *this* part of the subject, we shall be constrained once and again to trouble him with detailed specimens of the contents of ℵ B, &c., in proof of the justice of what we have been alleging. We venture to assure him, without a particle of hesitation, that ℵ B D are *three of the most scandalously corrupt copies extant:*–exhibit *the most shamefully mutilated* texts which are anywhere to be met with:–have become, by whatever process (for their history is wholly unknown), the depositories of the largest amount of *fabricated readings,* ancient *blunders,* and *intentional perversions of Truth,*–which are discoverable in any known copies of the Word of God.

But in fact take a single page of any ordinary copy of the Greek Testament,–Bp. Lloyd's edition, suppose. Turn to page 184. It contains ten verses of S. Luke's Gospel, ch. viii. 35 to 44. Now, proceed to collate those ten verses. You will make the notable discovery that, within those narrow limits, by codex D alone the text has been depraved 53 times, resulting in no less than 103 corrupt readings, 93 *of which are found only in* D. The words omitted by D are 40: the words added are 4. Twenty-five words have been substituted for others, and 14 transposed. Variations of case, tense, &c., amount to 16; and the phrase of the Evangelist has been departed from 11 times. Happily, the other four 'old uncials' are here available. And it is found that (within the same limits, and referred to the same test,) A exhibits 3 omissions, 2 of which are *peculiar to* A.–B omits 12 words, 6 of which are *peculiar to* B: substitutes 3 words: transposes 4: and exhibits 6 lesser changes–2 of them being its own peculiar property.–ℵ has 5 readings (affecting 8 words) *peculiar to itself.* Its omissions are 7: its additions 2: its substitutions, 4: 2 words are transposed; and it exhibits 4 lesser discrepancies,–C has 7 readings (affecting 15 words) *peculiar to itself.* Its omissions are 4: its additions, 7: its substitutions, 7: its words transposed, 7. It has 2 lesser discrepancies, and it alters the Evangelist's phrases 4 times.

But (we shall be asked) what amount of *agreement,* in respect of 'Various Readings,' is discovered to subsist between these 5 codices? for *that,* after all, is the practical question. We answer,–A has been already shown to stand alone twice: B, 6 times: ℵ, 8 times: C, 15 times; D, 93 times.–We have further to state that A B stand together by themselves once: B ℵ, 4 times: B C, 1: B D, 1: ℵ C, 1: C D, 1.–A ℵ C conspire 1: B ℵ C, 1: B ℵ D, 1: A B ℵ C, *once* (viz. in reading ἐρώτησεν, which Tischendorf admits to be a corrupted reading): B ℵ C D, also *once.*–The 5 'old uncials' therefore (A B ℵ C D) combined, and again stand apart, with singular impartiality.–Lastly, they are *never once* found to be in accord in respect of *any single 'various Reading.'*–Will any one, after a candid survey of the premises, deem us unreasonable, if we avow that such a specimen of the *concordia discors* which everywhere prevails between the oldest uncials, but which especially characterizes ℵ B D, indisposes us greatly to suffer their unsupported authority to determine for us the Text of Scripture?" (B)

*See "The Traditional Text Of The Holy Gospels Vindicated And Established By John William Burgon Arranged, Compiled, And Edited By Edward Miller 1896 London George Bell And Sons Cambridge: Deighton, Bell And Co."

**See See Eusebius's Ecclesiastical History book 3 chapter 37. Eusebius, A.D. 259 to A.D. 340)

***See "book 5 chapter 28 of "The Ecclesiastical History Of Eusebius Pamphilus, Bishop Of Cesarea, In Palestine." Translated From The Original, With An Introduction, By Christian Frederick Crusé And An Historical View Of The Council Of Nice, By Isaac Boyle. 1850. Ninth Edition. New York: Stanford & Swords, 137 Broadway."

****See "The Identity Of The New Testament Text By Wilbur N. Pickering 1977 Thomas Nelson Inc., Publishers"

(A) Quoted From: "The Ante-Nicene Fathers. Translations Of The Writings Of The Fathers Down To A.D. 325. By Alexander Roberts, And James Donaldson, Editors American Reprint Of The Edinburgh Edition. Revised And Chronologically Arranged, With Brief Prefaces And Occasional Notes, By A. Cleveland Coxe. Volume I. The Apostolic Fathers. – Justin Martyr. – Irenæus. 1903. New York: Charles Scribner's Sons."

(B) Quoted From: "The Revision Revised. Three Articles Reprinted From The 'Quarterly Review. I. The New Greek Text. II. The New English Version. III. Westcott And Hort's New Textual Theory. To Which Is Added A Reply To Bishop Ellicott's Pamphlet In Defence Of The Revisers And Their Greek Text Of The New Testament: Including A Vindication Of The Traditional Reading Of 1 Timothy III. 16. By John William Burgon 1883. John Murry, Albemarle Street."

Historical Attestation For The Bible Only

The greatest cry in the Protestant Reformation was: "The Bible Only", that is, The Bible is the only standard and only guide to Christian doctrine, truth, and thought. This however has been challenged by people who claim and assert that Christianity is based on tradition not Scripture, and that it was the authority of the Christian Church, by the power of tradition of authority to determined which Books make up The Canon, and this was done, so they say, not under the Apostles, but under those they deemed their successors. The question we must now ask is, is there any form of truth to any of those beliefs and assertions? The answer is: No, both as Scripture has shown and as early Christianity also declares.

First: Did Christians read the Scriptures from the very beginning?

We read from Clement of Rome (A.D. 30 to A.D. 100) in his "Epistle To The Corinthians" the following: "Ye are contentious brethren, and zealous for things which pertain not unto salvation. Look into the holy Scriptures, which are the true words of the Holy Ghost. Ye know that nothing unjust or counterfeit is written in them." Part 45. "Take into your hands the epistle of the blessed Paul the apostle. What did he first write to you at the beginning of the Gospel." Part 47 "Ye, know, beloved, ye know full well the holy Scriptures ; and have thoroughly searched into the oracles of God. Call them, therefore, to your remem-brance." Part 53 of "The Epistle Of Clement To The Corinthians." (H)

And from Polycarp (A.D. 65 to A.D. 155) in his "Epistle to the Philippians" we read: "For I trust that ye are well exercised in the holy Scriptures, and nothing is hid from you." Part 12 of "The Epistle Of Polycarp To The Philippians." (H)

Chrysostom: 'Let us not neglect the reading of the Holy Scriptures, for that is a devise of the devil, which forbids us to behold the treasure lest we should thereby be enriched.' (B)

Augustine: "The Scriptures of the Old and New Testaments, having been confirmed in the Apostles' time, and since by the Bishops who succeeded them, and the churches which have been propagated throughout the world, have been placed as it were upon a high throne, to which every faithful and godly understanding must be subject." (G)

Second: Did Christians only consider that which was written to be of authority?

Irenæus in the second century states: "We have received the method of our salvation from no others but from them by whom the Gospel came to us, which Gospels the Apostles first preached, but afterwards, by the will of God, delivered in writing, to be for the future the pillar and foundation of our faith." (A)

Chrysostom from the fourth and fifth centuries in his "Homilies": "All Christians ought to have recourse to *the Scriptures.* For at this time, since heresy has infected the churches, the *divine Scriptures alone* can afford a proof of genuine Christianity, and a refuge to those who are desirous of arriving at the true faith. Formerly it might have been ascertained by various means, which was the true church ; but at present, there is no other method left to those who are willing to discover the true church of Christ, but by *the Scriptures alone.* And why? Be-cause heresy has all outward observance in common with her. If a man, therefore, be desirous of knowing the true church, how will he be able to do it amidst so great a resemblance, but by the Scriptures alone? Wherefore our Lord, foreseeing that such a great con-fusion of things would take place in the latter days, orders the Christian to have recourse to *nothing but the Scriptures.* Let us not attend to the opinions of the many;—especially as we possess THE MOST EXACT AND PERFECT RULE AND STANDARD by which to regulate our several inquiries--I mean the REGULATIONS OF THE DI-VINE LAWS. Therefore I could wish that all of you would neglect what this or that man asserts for truth, and that you would investigate all these things in *the Scriptures.*" (G)

From Origen from the third century we learn: "In the two Testaments every word that appertaineth unto God may be sought and discussed, and out of them all knowledge of things is to be derived. But, if anything remains which Divine Scripture does not determine, no other third Scripture ought to be received to authorise knowledge." (I)

Third: Did Christians consider that any Church body or counsel had authority to determine Doctrine for them?

Cyprian from the third century states: "Whence have you that tradition ? Comes it from the authority of the Lord and of the Gospel, or from the Apostolic epistles ? For God hath testified that we are to do those things which are written. If it be commanded in the Gospels, or contained in the epistles, or Acts of the Apostles, then let us believe it is a divine and holy tradition." (A)

Tertullian from the third century states: "As for Hermogenes, let his shop or library produce the word of God ; if he be unable to produce the written word, in substantiation of his tenets, let him fear the woe destined to those who either add or take from it." (A)

Fourth: Did Christian teachers of Doctrine state that the Holy Scriptures were alone to be the rule of faith, and that people should only believe what the Scriptures demonstrate to be true?

Cyril of Jerusalem from the fourth century states: "Respecting the divine and holy mysteries of the faith, not even a tittle ought to be delivered without the authority of THE HOLY SCRIPTURES. Neither ought any thing to be propounded, on the basis of mere credibility, or through the medium of plausible ratiocination. Neither yet repose the slightest con-fidence in the bare assertions of me your Catechist, unless you shall receive from THE HOLY SCRIPTURES full demonstration of the matters propounded. For the security of our faith depends, not upon verbal trickery, but upon demonstration from THE HOLY SCRIPTURES." Athanasius from the fourth century states: "The holy and divine inspired SCRIPTURES are sufficient for the declaration of the truth." And he declares: "Let a person solely learn the matters, which are set forth in the SCRIPTURES : for the demonstra-tions, contained in them, are, in order to the settling of this point, quite sufficient and complete." (C)

Basil from the fourth century declares: "It is a manifested apostasy from the faith, and a clear proof of arrogance, either to disregard any mat-ter of THE THINGS WHICH ARE WRITTEN, or to in-troduce argumentatively any matter of THE THINGS WHICH ARE NOT WRITTEN." And he states: "THE THINGS WHICH ARE WRITTEN believe : THE THINGS WHICH ARE NOT WRITTEN seek not after." Jerome from the fourth and fifth centuries states: "As we deny not THE THINGS WHICH ARE WRITTEN : so THE THINGS WHICH ARE NOT WRIT-TEN we reject." And he states: "Learn, then, in the DEVINE SCRIPTURES, through which ALONE you can understand the full will of God," (C)

Augustine from the fourth and fifth centuries declares: "Demonstrate, from any one of THE CANONICAL APOSTLES AND PROPHETS, the truth of what Cyprian has written to Jubaianus: and I should then have no room for contradiction. But now, since what you produce is NOT CANONICAL ; through the liberty to which the Lord hath called us, I receive not the decision." (C)

Fifth: Did the early Christians consider that the Apostles were the only ones to give us the Holy Scriptures?

Basil from the fourth century states: "We have received it from our fathers, but this is not enough for us, for they followed the authority of the Scriptures, making its testimonies the principle on which to build." Austin from the fifth century declares: "Neither ought I now to allege the Nicene Coun-cil, nor you that of Ariminum, for neither of us is bound by the authority of the one or the other. Let us both contest with the authorities of Scripture, which are witnesses common to both." Cyril from the fifth century states: "It behoveth us not to deliver the very least thing of the sacred mysteries of faith without the Holy Scriptures. This is the security of our faith— not what is delivered from our own inventions, but what is demonstrated from the Holy Scrip-tures." Jerome from the fifth century states: "those things which, without the authorities and testimonies of the Scripture, men invent of their own heads, as for Apostolic tradition they are smitten by the sword of God." he also states: "It comes from a demoniacal spirit, that men follow the sophisms of human minds, and think anything divine, that wants the authority of Scripture." (A)

Chrysostom states: "The Philosophers speak obscurely, but the Apostles and Prophets make all things delivered by them clear and manifest; and, as the common teachers of the world, have so expounded all things, that every man may, of himself, by bare reading, learn those things which are spoken." (N)

Sixth: Did the early Christians spread the books of the New Testament around as they preached Christianity?

Eusebius (A.D. 259 To A.D. 340) in his "Ecclesiastical History" book 3 chapter 37 reveals to us how copies of the Gospels were spread about at a very early time by Christians in vicinities throughout the whole world. We read: "afterwards leav-ing their country, they performed the office of evangelists to those who had not yet heard the faith, whilst, with a noble ambition to proclaim Christ, they delivered to them the books of the holy gospels. After laying the foundation of the faith in foreign parts as the particular object of their mission," (J)

We read in: Book 4 Chapter 33 of "The Ecclesiastical History Of Socrates Scholasticus (Born A.D. 379 or, 380)." the following: "Ulfilas, their bishop at that time, invented the Gothic letters, and translat-ing the Sacred Scriptures into their own lan-guage, undertook to instruct these barbarians in the Divine oracles." (K)

Chrysostom states: "Where is the philosophy of Plato and Pythagoras? Ex-tinguished. Where is the teaching of the tent-maker and fisherman? Not only in Judæa, but also among the barbarians, as ye have this day perceived, it shines more brilliantly than the sun itself. Scythians, and Thracians, Samaritans, Moors and Indians, and those who inhabit the extremes of the world, possess this teaching translated into their own language;" (L)

Augustine reveals: "Hence it hath come to pass, that the scriptures of God (which is the remedy for such grievous disorders of the human will), proceed from one language, commodiously fitted for the dissemination through the globe, and diffused far and wide by the various tongues of its interpreters, hath become known to all people for their salvation; which when they read, they desire nothing else but to find out the thoughts and will of God, ac-cording to which we believe that such men as they were spoken." (M)

Seventh: Did the early Christians consider that everyone should have free use of the Holy Scriptures despite what their position was within the Church?

We read from John Chrysostom (around A.D. 347 to A.D. 407) made Bishop of Constantinople in A.D. 398 in homily nine on Colossians (See Colossians 3:16-17) where he states: "Hearken, I entreat you, all ye that are careful for this life, and procure books that will be medicines for the soul. If ye will not any other, yet get you at least the New Testament, the Apostles, the Acts, the Gospels, for your constant teachers. If grief befall thee, dive into them as into a chest of medicines ; take thence comfort of thy trouble, be it loss, or death, or bereavement of relations ; or rather dive not into them merely, but take them wholly to thee ; keep them in mind. This is the cause of all evils, the not knowing of the Scriptures." (D)

Chrysostom in his Homily on Lazarus states: "I do always exhort, and will never cease to exhort you, that you will not here only attend to those things which are spoken; but, when you are at home, you continually busy yourselves in reading the Holy Scriptures, which practice also, I have not ceased to urge upon them who come privately to me. For, let no man say, 'Alas, I am taken up with lawful causes, I am employed in public affairs, I follow my trade, I maintain a wife and children, and have a great charge to look to; it is not for me to read the Scriptures, but for them which have cast off the world, which have taken up the solitary tops of mountains for their dwellings, which live this contemplative kind of life continually.' What sayest thou, O man? Is it not for thee to turn over the Scriptures, because thou art distracted with many cares? Nay, then it is for thee more then for them ; for they do not so much need the help of the Scriptures as thou who art tossed in the midst of the waves of worldly business." (N)

Jerome states: "It is for the whole people that the Apostles wrote. The laity ought to abound in the knowledge of the Holy Scriptures." (N)

Jerome states: "Ignorance of the Scrip-tures is ignorance of Christ." (O)

Irenaeus in book five, chapter eight of his book "Against Heresies" states: "Now the law has figuratively predicted all these, delineating man by the [various] animals: whatsoever of these, says [the Scriptures], have a double hoof and ruminate, it proclaims as clean; but whatsoever of them do not possess one or other of these [properties], it sets aside by themselves as unclean. Who then are the clean? Those who make their way by faith steadily towards the Father and the Son; for this is denoted by the steadiness of those which divide the hoof; and they meditate day and night upon the words of God, that they may be adorned with good works: for this is the meaning of the ruminates. The unclean, however, are those which do neither divide the hoof nor ruminate; that is, those persons who have neither faith in God, nor do meditate on His words: and such is the abomination of the Gentiles. But as to those animals which do indeed chew the cud, but have not the double hoof, and are themselves unclean, we have in them a figurative description of the Jews, who certainly have the words of God in their mouth, but who do not fix their rooted stedfastness in the Father and in the Son; wherefore they are an unstable generation. For those animals which have the hoof all in one piece easily slip; but those that have it divided are more sure-footed, their cleft hoofs succeeding each other as they advance, and the one hoof supporting the other, In like manner, too, those are unclean which have the double hoof but do not ruminate: this is plainly an indication of all heretics, and of those who do not meditate on the words of God, neither are adorned with works of righteousness: to whom also the Lord says. "Why call ye me Lord, Lord, and do not the things which I say to you?" For men of this stamp do indeed say that they believe in the Father and the Son, but they never meditate as they should upon the things of God, neither are they adorned with works of righteousness; but, as I have already observed, they have adopted the lives of swine and of dogs, giving themselves over to filthiness, to gluttony, and recklessness of all sorts. Justly, therefore, did the apostle call all such "carnal" and "animal," –[all those, namely], who through their own unbelief and luxury do not receive the Devine Spirit, and in their various phases cast out from themselves the life-giving Word, and walk stupidly after their own lusts: the prophets, too, spake of them as beasts of burden and wild beasts; custom likewise has viewed them in the light of cattle and irrational creatures; and the law has pronounced them unclean." (Q)

Eighth: Did the early Christians mention the names of the Apostles?

We get a list of the inspired writers of the New Testament from Origen

(From A.D. 185 to A.D. 253-254) in his fourteenth homily on Genesis we read: "Isaac therefore dug Wells, and the Followers of Isaac dug too, The Followers of Isaac are Matthew, Mark, Luke, John. The Followers of Isaac are Peter, James, and Jude. The Apostle Paul is a Follower of Isaac. For all these dig the Wells of the New Testament." (E)

We get a further list from the same Origen in his Commentary on Joshua we read: "When our Lord Jesus Christ came in the flesh, (He whose advent Jesus the son of Nun prefigured,) He made his apostles walk as priests, bearing the trumpets of the grand and heavenly doctrine of the preached word. It was Matthew who, in his Gospel, first sounded the sacerdotal clarion. Then Mark, then Luke, then John, each in succession blew his trumpet. After them Peter burst forth with the two trumpets of his epistles, Then comes James, and then Jude. Then comes John, to send forth, in addition to his previous blast, fresh sounds of his trumpet by his epistles and Apocalypse and so also does Luke, in putting forth his Acts of the Apostles. Last comes, in his turn, he who said, (1 Cor. iv. 9,) 'I think that God hath set forth us the apostles last.' When he wakes the thunders of his trumpets by his fourteen epistles, he overturned from their very foundation the walls of Jericho,—all the war-engines of idolatry, all the tenets of false philosophy." (F)

Jerome (About A.D. 347 to A.D. 420) in his Letter to Paulinus speaks thus: "The New Testament I will briefly deal with. Matthew, Mark, Luke and John are the Lord's team of four, the true cherubim or store of knowledge. With them the whole body is full of eyes, they glitter as sparks, they run and return like lightning, their feet are straight feet, and lift up, their backs also are winged, ready to fly in all directions. They hold together each by each and are interwoven one with another : like wheels within wheels they roll along and go whithersoever the breath of the Holy Spirit wafts them. The apostle Paul writes to seven churches (for the eighth epistle—that to the Hebrews—is not generally counted in the others.) He instructs Timothy and Titus ; he intercedes with Philemon for his runaway slave. Of him I think it better to say nothing than to write inadequately. The Acts of the Apostles seem to relate a mere unvarnished narrative descriptive of the infancy of the newly born church ; but when once we realize that their author is Luke the physician whose praise is in the gospel, we shall see that all his words are medicine for the sick soul. The apostles James, Peter, John, and Jude, have published seven epistles at once spiritual and to the point, short and long, short that is in words but lengthy in substance so that there are few indeed who do not find themselves in the dark when they read them. The apocalypse of John has as many mysteries as words. In saying this I have said less that the book deserves. All praise of it is inadequate ; manifold meanings lie hid in its every word." (P)

(A) Quoted in: "Popery Unmasked ; Being Thirty Conversations Between Mr. Daylight And Mr. Twilight, In Which The Peculiar Doctrines, Morales, Governments, And Usages Of The Romish Church Are Truthfully Stated From Her Own Duly Authorised Works, And Impartially Tried By God's Word, The Only Unerring Rule Of Doctrine And Duty. By Henry Woodcock 1862 London: Published By Richard Davison, Conference Offices, Sutton-Street, Commercial-Road, May Be Had Of Primitive Methodist Ministers. Pages 25-26

(B) Quoted in: "Our Brief Against Rome By Charles Stuteville Isaacson 1905 London The Religious Tract Society Page 197

(C) Quoted In: "Facts And Assertions: Or A Brief And Plain Exhibition Of The Incongruity Of The Peculiar Doctrines Of The Church Of Rome With Those, Both Of The Sacred Scriptures, And Of The Early Writers Of The Christian Church Catholic. By George Stanley Faber 1831. London: Printed For C. J. G. & F. Rivington, Booksellers to the Society for Promoting Christian Knowledge, St. Paul's Church-Yard, And Waterloo-Place, Pall-Mall. Pages 35-37

(D) Quoted From: "A Library Of The Fathers Of The Holy Catholic Church, Anterior To The Division Of The East And West. Translated By The Members Of The English Church. 1879. Oxford, James Parker And Co., And Rivingtons, London, Oxford, And Cambridge. The Homilies Of S. John Chrysostom Archbishop Of Constantinople On The Epistles Of S. Paul The Apostle To The Philippians, Colossians, And Thessalonians. New Edition Revised.

Delineation Of Roman Catholicism, Drawn From The Authentic And Acknowledged Standards Of The Church Of Rome: Namely, Her Creeds, Catechisms, Decisions Of Councils, Papal Bulls, Roman Catholic Writers, The Records Of History, Ect. Ect.: In Which The Peculiar Doctrines, Morals, Government, And Usages Of The Church Of Rome, Are Stated, Treated At Large, And Confuted. By Charles Elliott 1841 New-York: Published By George Lain, For The Methodist Episcopal Church, At The Conference Office, 200 Mulberry-Street. J. Collord, Printer. Volume I

The Church Of Rome Examined: Or, Can I Ever Enter The Church Of Rome, So Long As I Believe The Whole Bible? A Question Submitted To The Conscience Of Every Christian Reader. Translated From The French Of The C. Malan. By The John Cormack, 1840. London: James Nisbet And

Co. Berners S J. Johnstone, Edinburgh ; William Collins, Glasgow ; W. Curry, & Co. Dublin ; And M'Come, Belfast.

(G) Quoted From: A Dissertation On The Rule Of Faith; Delivered At Cincinnati, Ohio, At The Annual Meeting Of The American Bible Society, And Published At Their Request. By Gardiner Spring. 1844. New York: Leavitt, Trow, & Co., 194 Broadway.

(H) Quoted From: "A Translation Of The Epistles Of Clement, Of Rome, Polycarp, And Ignatius, And The First Apology Of Justin Martyr, With An Introduction And Brief Notes Illustrative Of The Ecclesiastical History Of The First Two Centuries. By Temple Chevallier Edited By Wm. R. Whittingham 1846 New-York: Henry M. Onderdonk & Co., 25 John-ST."

(I) Quoted From: "Dr. Wiseman's Popish Literary Blunders Exposed. By Charles Hastings Collette. 1860. London. Arthur Hall, Virtue & Co., 25, Paternoster-Row.

(J) Quoted From: "An Ecclesiastical History To The Twentieth Year Of The Reign Of Constantine, Being The 324TH Of The Christian Æra. By Eusebius, Surnamed Pamphilus, Bishop Of Cæsarea. Translated By C. F. Crusè 1842 London: Samuel Bagster And Sons, Paternoster Row; At the Warehouse For Bibles, New Testaments, Prayer Books, Psalters, And Concordances, In Ancient And Modern Languages.

(K) Quoted From: "Book 4 Chapter 33 of "The Ecclesiastical History Of Socrates Scholasticus (Born A.D. 379 or, 380)." In "A Select Library Of The Nicene And Post-Nicene Fathers Of The Christian Church. Second Series. Translated Into English With Prolegomena And Explanatory Notes Under The Editorial Supervision Of Henry Wace And Philip Schaff. Volume II. Socrates, Sozomenus : Church Historians. 1891. Oxford: Parker And Company. New York: The Christian Literature Company."

(L) Quoted From: "Saint Chrysostom His Life And Times A Sketch Of The Church And The Empire In The Fourth Century. By W. R. W. Stephens. 1872. London John Murry, Albemarle Street.

(M) Quoted From: "A Disputation On Holy Scripture, Against The Papists, Especially Bellarmine And Stapleton. By William Whitaker. Translated And Edited For The Parker Society By William Fitzgerald 1849. Cambridge: Printed At The University Press.

(N) Quoted From: "A Protestant's Appeal To The Douay Bible, And Other

Roman Catholic Standards, In Support Of The Doctrines Of The Reformation. By John Jenkins. 1853. Fourth Edition. Montreal: Wesleyan Book Depot, Great St. James Street."

(O) Quoted From: "A Plain Protestant Manuel, Or, Certain Plain Sermons On The Scriptures, The Church, And The Sacraments, &c. &c. &c. In Which The Corruptions Of The Romish Church Are Evidently Set Forth. By John Wood Warter 1851. London: Francis & John Rivington, St. Paul's Church Yard, And Waterloo Place."

(E) Quoted From: "The Canon Of The New Testament Vindicated; In Answer To The Objections Of J. Toland, In His Amyntor. By John Richardson 1619 London: Printed By W. Bowyer, For Richard Sare, Near Gray's-Inn-Gate In Holborn."

(F) Quoted From: The Canon Of The Holy Scriptures From The Double Point Of View Of Science And Of Faith. By L. Gaussen 1862 London: James Nisbet And Co., 21 Berners Street.

The Canon Of The Old And New Testament Ascertained, Or, The Bible Complete Without The Apocrypha And Unwritten Traditions. By Archibald Alexander 1851 Philadelphia: Presbyterian Board Of Publications, No. 265 Chestnut Street."

(P) A Select Library Of Nicene And Post-Nicene Fathers Of The Church Of Christ. Second Series. Translated Into English With Prolegomena And Explanatory Notes Under The Editorial Supervision Of Philip Schaff And Henry Wace. Volume VI. 1893. St. Jerome: Letters And Select Works: New York: The Christian Literature Company. Oxford And London: Parker & Company.

(Q) Ante-Nicene Christian Library: Translations Of The Writings Of The Fathers Down To A.D. 325. Edited By Alexander Roberts, And James Donaldson, Vol. IX. Irenæus, Vol., II. –Hippolytus, Vol. II. –Fragments Of The Third Century. Edinburgh: T. & T. Clark, 38, George Street. MDCCCLXIX.

Fathers Of The Catholic Church. A Brief Examination Of The "Falling Away" Of The Church In The First Three Centuries. By E. J. Waggoner. 1888 Pacific Press Publishing Company.

HOW AND WHY HUMANITY IS SINFUL

Holy Scripture makes it very clear that we are all sinners without exception (See Romans 3:23; Ecclesiastes 7:20; Jeremiah 13:23), and the wages of sin is death (See Romans 6:23; Isaiah 64:6), which is why our sins must be purged from us through Christ Jesus our Lord for us to receive eternal life, as we will discuss in a latter chapter. The question becomes now however is, How is it that we are all sinners? And we find that the answer is that since God hath given all the ability to have freedom of choice (See Deuteronomy 30:19; Joshua 24:15; Malachi 3:6), we all have the ability to choose in one way or another to do good or evil, and so, since this freedom of choice both extended to the Devil and also to the first of us Adam and Eve, we can ascertain what happened as anyone who has read The Bible should know, that is, the serpent, which is the Devil choose to tempted Eve in the Garden of Eden, and she sadly gave into this temptation of which Adam also participated, and so, seeing that eating the forbidden fruit was a sin (Compare Genesis 2:17; Romans 6:23), sin was thusly introduced into this world.

Now consider however, for Holy Scripture makes it very clear that no-one takes on the sin of another human being, for all are responsible for their own actions (See Ezekiel 18:20; also Romans 5:14). The question that then arises of course is, If we do not inherently have the sin of Adam, then how are we all sinners? (See Romans 3:23; Romans 3:10-12) And the Bible reveals, that we have all sinned because we have a nature of sin, for as we learn, since children are brought up in the way they should go (See Proverbs 22:6), and since Adam and Eve who had sinned, and thus had a nature to sin (See Jeremiah 17:9; Jeremiah 13:23; Ecclesiastes 7:20), they would only ever bring up children to be sinners, for they would no doubt sin at times, and thus, in this way, passed on sin through teaching their children to sin, which would go on all the way down throughout the centuries of time through their descendants (See Psalm 51:5; Genesis 5:3; Ecclesiastes 7:20; Ecclesiastes 8:11; Isaiah 48:8), and so, in this way, we suffer from the first sin of the first of us, yet let us not despair, for Christ Jesus our Lord is greater then our nature, for He was and is without sin (See 1 Peter 2:21-22; Hebrews 4:15), and we that follow Him will not only receive eternal life through Him (See John 3:16-18; Romans 6:23), but we will receive His sinless nature (Consider 2 Peter 1:4; Romans 13:14; Galatians 2:20). Amen.

Now let us unpack some these texts that we have pointed out from Holy Writ. And so, we read that we re all sinners: "For all have sinned, and come short of the glory of God; (Romans 3:23) For there is not a just man upon earth, that doeth good, and sinneth not. (Ecclesiastes 7:20) Can the Ethiopian change his skin, or the leopard his spots? then may ye also do good, that are accustom to do evil. (Jeremiah 13:23) And because of our sin we are under a sentence of death, for we are separated from God who Himself is the only giver of life which is through Christ Jesus our Lord. "For the wages of sin is death; but the gift of God is eternal life through Jesus Christ our Lord. (Romans 6:23) For "we are all an unclean thing, and all our righteousnesses are as filthy rags; and we all do fade as a leaf; and our iniquities, like the wind, have taken us away. (Isaiah 64:6) But your iniquities have separated between you and your God, and your sins have hid his face from you, that he will not hear. (Isaiah 59:2)

Now consider that we all without exception or reservation have freedom of choice as we read: "And if it seem evil unto you to serve the LORD, choose you this day whom ye will serve; whether the gods which your fathers served that were on the other side of the flood, or the gods of the Amorites, in whose land ye dwell: but as for me and my house, we will serve the LORD. (Joshua 24:15) I call heaven and earth to record this day against you, that I have set before you life and death, blessing and cursing: therefore choose life, that both thou and thy seed may live: (Deuteronomy 30:19). And seeing that The LORD hath said: "For I am the LORD I change not; (Malachi 3:6) we can then know that freedom of choice has always been available to all, both to the first of us, that is, Adam and Eve and also to the bringer of evil and death, the Devil.

Now consider that we have not inherited the sin of Adam that cast him and Eve out of the Garden of Eden, for "The soul that sinneth, it shall die. The son shall not bear the iniquity of the father, neither shall the father bear the iniquity of the son: the righteousness of the righteous shall be upon him, and the wickedness of the wicked shall be upon him. (Ezekiel 18:20) Therefore, seeing that we have not inherited the sin of Adam, the question then is, How is it that we are all sinners? And the answer is that we inherit the propensity to sin from Adam and Even, for we being their descendants, and they bringing up children, they could only ever bringing up children to be like themselves, which means since they were sinners and had the nature to sin, they would most probably sin at times, and thus, in this way teach their children to sin (as well as the Devil giving temptations) and so, in this way, we are all indeed full of sin, For "the scripture hath concluded all under sin, that the promise by faith of Jesus Christ might be given to them that believe. (Galatians 3:22 See 1 Corinthians 15:3-4). And so we read concerning that we inherit the nature and propensity to sin because of Adam and Eve the following: "Train up a child in the way he should go: and when he is old, he will not depart from it. (Proverbs 22:6) Who can bring a clean thing out of an unclean? not one. (Job 14:4) And Adam lived an hundred and thirty years, and begat a son in his own likeness, and after his image; and called his name Seth: (Genesis 5:3) And so, in this way, we all have and receive a sinful nature through the free choice and actions of Adam and Eve, even though we do not inherit the actual sin that they themselves committed. Amen.

HOW GOD REMOVES OUR SINS THROUGH JESUS CHRIST

How is it that we are saved in Christianity? We know that the death of Christ Jesus our Lord upon The Cross caused us to be saved (See 1 Corinthians 15:3-4; Isaiah 53:1-12; Acts 16:30-31), but how exactly? This is what we are now going to discuss in this chapter specifically, by the grace, mercy, and leading of God, and if it be His will. Amen.

We learn from Holy Writ, that we are all of us sinners without exception (See Romans 3:23; Galatians3:22; Ecclesiastes 7:20; Jeremiah 13:23; Romans 3:10-12), and as sinners we are completely separated from God to the point that He will not even hear us (See Isaiah 59:2), for we are unable to work our way into heaven (See Isaiah 64:6; Luke 17:10), therefore it is a free gift of God of grace, and justification, and righteousness (See Romans 5:15-18; Ephesians 2:8-10; Romans 5:1-2; Romans 4:3,5-8,20-25), for it is God who reconciles us to Himself through the death of Christ Jesus our Lord (See Isaiah 59:2; 2 Corinthians 5:18-19; Romans 5:10; Ephesians 2:16-18; Colossians 1:14,20-21; Hebrews 2:17; Hebrews 7:27; Daniel 9:24; Isaiah 53:1-12), of which we die through Christ Jesus our Lord through Baptism (See Romans 6:3-8), and then the penalty of sin which is death is paid, for the penalty has been fulfilled (Compare Romans 6:23; Romans 6:7), and we remain in death through Christ Jesus our Lord, and thus free from sin (See Colossians 3:3-4; Galatians 2:20; Romans 6:7; 1 John 4:9), as long as we do not become separated from Him by departing from Him (See John 15:1-7), which is our free choice (Consider John 3:16-18; Deuteronomy 30:19; Joshua 24:15; Revelation 22:17).

And so, being in Christ through the crucifixion and death of Baptism

(Compare Romans 6:3-8; Galatians 2:20; Also See John 15:1-7; Galatians 3:26-27; Colossians 2:12-13; Colossians 3:3-4), and God being within Christ as well (See 2 Corinthians 5:18-19), we are then reconciled to God through Christ Jesus our Lord who is our mediator (See 1 Timothy 2:5; Hebrews 2:17; Hebrews 7:25). Therefore, we must die through Christ through Baptism (See Romans 6:3-8), both because this is how God reconciles us to Himself (See 2 Corinthians 5:18-19; Romans 5:10) because God will not hear sinners (See Isaiah 59:2), and because no one can pay for another persons transgressions (See Ezekiel 18:20), therefore again we die through Christ through Baptism (See Romans 6:3-8), and then the penalty of sin which is death is paid (Compare Romans 6:23; Romans 6:7), and we remain in death through Christ Jesus our Lord, and thus free from sin (Colossians 3:3-4; Galatians 2:20; Romans 6:7).

Furthermore, We learn also, that eternal life is bestowed upon us through The Words of Christ Jesus our Lord (See John 6:53-54,63), for through His Words we abide in Him (See John 6:56,63) and His Words make us clean (Compare John 15:3; John 15:1-7; John 6:53-54,63; also Ephesians 5:26; John 5:24), His Words being The Bible (Compare John 14:26; John 16:13; John 15:26; Hebrews 2:3; John 17:17; 1 Timothy 2:3-4; 1 Thessalonians 2:13; 2 Corinthians 1:13; Acts 13:27; Jeremiah 36:1-4; John 6:63; Ephesians 6:17; 1 Corinthians 2:13; John 14:24; Ephesians 6:17; 2 Timothy 3:16-17; 2 Peter 3:15-16; 1 John 5:13; John 20:30-31; Isaiah 34:16; Titus 1:3; John 10:27-28; Compare 2 Corinthians 1:13; Titus 1:3; 1 Thessalonians 2:13; Ephesians 6:17; Compare Matthew 7:21; John 14:24; John 6:63; Ephesians 6:17; Compare Hebrews 2:3; 2 Corinthians 1:13; 1 John 5:13; John 20:30-31; John 6:63; Ephesians 6:17),

Which Words cause us to have belief in Him (See John 20:30-31; 1 John 5:13), which is imperative, for we will not receive eternal life without belief in Christ Jesus our Lord (See John 3:16-18; Romans 8:1; John 5:24; Romans 4:3,5-8,11,20-25; John 6:28-29; Romans 10:9-10; Also 1 Timothy 2:5; John 14:6; Romans 1:17; Mark 16:15-16), for we receive the free gift of God of grace, and justification, and righteousness through belief in God (Compare Romans 5:15-18; Ephesians 2:8-10; Romans 5:1-2; Romans 4:3,5-8,20-25). For we are made a child of God through faith in Christ Jesus our Lord (See Galatians 3:26-27; Consider 1 John 3:10), which is very important, for we are to be made a New Creature (See 2 Corinthians 5:17; Galatians 6:15; Ephesians 2:8-16) and New Man (See Ephesians 4:22-24; Colossians 3:8-10; Romans 6:6), which is accomplished by the Old Man being crucified and dying through the waters of baptism (See Romans 6:3-8), and then we are reborn, that is Born Again (See John 3:3-7), which is accomplished by the Waters of Baptism (See John 3:5; Acts 22:16; Acts 8:36; Acts 8:38; Acts

10:47; also Romans 6:3-11; also Compare Acts 22:16; Revelation 1:5), and by receiving The Spirit of God who comes to the children of God (See John 3:5; Luke 11:13; Galatians 3:26; Also See John 7:38-39; Luke 11:13; Romans 8:1-2; Romans 8:9-10; Galatians 3:26; Also See Galatians 3:26-27; Romans 8:15-16,23; Galatians 4:5; Ephesians 1:5), and also through The Words of God, The Bible (See 1 Peter 1:23-25; Compare John 3:5; Ephesians 5:26; Compare 1 John 5:1; John 20:30-31; 1 John 5:13; Also 1 John 2:29; Galatians 3:26-27).

We learn righteousness through The Bible (See 2 Timothy 3:16-17), which is important, for we are all unrighteous (See Romans 3:10-12), and the unrighteous will not enter the Kingdom of God (See 1 Corinthians 6:9), for only the righteous will enter into the Kingdom of God (Consider 1 Corinthians 6:9; Matthew 13:43; Matthew 25:34-37,46), which is important to understand, for we are unable to make ourselves righteous (See Isaiah 64:6; Isaiah 59:2; Luke 17:10), therefore God imputes righteousness unto us by belief in Him (See Romans 4:3,5-8,11,20-25; Romans 5:1-2; Also Romans 3:22,26; Galatians 3:6; James 2:23; Roans 10:9-10; Genesis 15:6), for it is His free gift (See Romans 5:15-17), and Christ Jesus our Lord cleanses us from all unrighteousness (See 1 John 1:9), thus we are free from condemnation (See John 3:15-18; Romans 8:1; John 5:24; Romans 5:16-18; Romans 8:13; Galatians 5:19-26).

It should be pointed out, that those who do righteousness are righteous (See 1 John 2:29; 1 John 3:7), while those who do unrighteousness are unrighteousness (See 1 Corinthians 6:9; 1 John 3:8-10), for you are either a Child of God through faith in Christ Jesus (See Galatians 3:26), or a child of the Devil (See 1 John 3:10). For says are Lord Jesus Christ: "He that is not with me is against me; and he that gathereth not with me scattereth abroad. (Matthew 12:30; See Romans 8:13; Galatians 5:19-26) For God so loved the world, that he gave his only begotten Son that whosoever believeth in him should not perish, but have everlasting life. For God sent not his Son into the world to condemn the world; but that the world through him might be saved. He that believeth on him is not condemned: but he that believeth not is condemned already, because he hath not believed in the name of the only begotten Son of God. (John 3:16-18) For I delivered unto you first of all that which I also received, how that Christ died for our sins according to the scriptures; And that he was buried, and that he rose again the third day according to the scriptures. (1 Corinthians 15:3-4)

This now brings us to the sacrificial atonement offering of Christ Jesus our Lord. For, as we learn through Holy Writ, The sacrifice of our Lord and

Savior Jesus Christ upon The Cross and His Blood reconciles us to God (See Leviticus 17:11; 2 Chronicles 29:24; Hebrews 10:1; Hebrews 10:1-12; 1 Corinthians 5:7; 1 Peter 1:18-19; John 1:29,36; Hebrews 13:11-13; Ephesians 1:7; Colossians 1:14,20), for His death, blood, and Words sanctifies us (See Hebrews 10:10; Hebrews 13:11-12; Hebrews 9:12-14; John 17:17; Ephesians 6:17; 1 Peter 1:2), and His resurrection and blood justifies us (See Romans 4:25; Romans 5:9), for His blood is what atones for our sins (Compare Leviticus 17:11; 2 Chronicles 29:24; Hebrews 10:1; Hebrews 10:1-12; 1 Corinthians 5:7; 1 Peter 1:18-19; John 1:29,36; Hebrews 13:11-13; Ephesians 1:7; Colossians 1:14,20; See Romans 5:11), the waters of Baptism representing His Blood (Compare Acts 22:16; Revelation 1:5; See Psalm 51:2; 1 John 1:7), which is why belief and baptism is necessary for salvation (See Mark 16:15-16).

The pure sacrificial lamb in The Old Testament and its blood were a shadow of the true atonement offering which was Christ Jesus our Lord (See Leviticus 17:11; 2 Chronicles 29:24; Hebrews 10:1-12; 1 Corinthians 5:7; 1 Peter 1:18-19; John 1:29,36; Hebrews 13:11-13; Ephesians 1:7; Colossians 1:14,20), which is why The Blood of Christ Jesus our Lord who is without sin (See 1 Peter 2:21-22; Hebrews 4:15) is The Most Important thing in the world, for through His Blood we are indeed reconciled to God (See Colossians 1:20), redeemed (See Colossians 1:14; Ephesians 1:7; Hebrews 9:12-14,22), sanctified (See Hebrews 13:12; Hebrews 9:13-14), justified (See Romans 5:9), cleansed and purified (See Hebrews 9:13-14,22; Acts 20:28; 1 John 1:7), and washed from our sins (Compare Acts 22:16; Revelation 1:5) through His atoning blood (See Romans 5:8-11; Leviticus 17:11; 2 Chronicles 29:24; Hebrews 10:1-12), that only needed to be offered once (See Hebrews 9:28; Hebrews 7:26-27; Hebrews 10:10-14), for through Him we are able to come to repentance (See Acts 5:31; Acts 11:18; Acts 3:19; Isaiah 1:18; Psalm 51:10; Acts 2:38; 1 John 1:7-10; 1 John 1:9; Acts 10:43; Romans 2:4; 2 Peter 3:9), and thus receive the Free gift of grace and justification and righteousness (See Romans 5:15-18; Ephesians 2:8-10; Compare Ephesians 3:7 Ephesians 4:7), for God forgives us of our sins (See Acts 10:43; 1 John 1:7-10; 1 John 2:1-3), and then command us to be perfect (See Colossians 1:28; Matthew 5:48; Philippians 3:15; 2 Corinthians 13:11; also See Isaiah 26:3; Psalm 51:10; Jeremiah 17:9; Isaiah 1:18; 1 John 1:7-10; Psalm 51:2; Acts 22:16; Revelation 1:5), which we learn through reading Holy Writ (See 2 Timothy 3:16-17), and then God works through us (See Philippians 2:13; 1 Corinthians 15:10; also Isaiah 48:17), while any evil is our own volition (See James 1:14), which is why good works do not bestow upon us merit, (See Luke 17:10), for again, it is God doing the good works through us (See Philippians 2:13), which is why belief is so vital to our salvation (See John 3:15-18), for God does not force belief upon us, we must choose (See Deuteronomy 30:19; Joshua 24:15), and we learn belief through reading and studying Holy Writ (See John 20:30-31; 1 John 5:13), which is The Sword of God (See Ephesians 6:17; John 6:63; 1 Corinthians 2:13).

For without belief we will not be saved (See John 3:15-18), and belief it should be pointed out, if you do not obey what God has stated to do in His Holy Words, then this is considered rebellion, which is considered that you do not believe (Compare Numbers 20:12; Numbers 20:24; Context Numbers 20:7-13; Numbers 20:23-24; Also See 1 Samuel 15:23), which is why our Lord and Savior Jesus Christ is the author of eternal salvation to all those who believe and obey Him (See Romans 6:16; Hebrews 5:9; John 6:28-29; Hebrews 11:8; John 3:15-18). For indeed, it is Christ Jesus our Lord who forgives us our sins and cleanses us of all unrighteousness through His Blood (See 1 Peter 1:18-20; Acts 20:28; Acts 10:43; 1 John 2:1-3; 1 John 1:7-10; Ephesians 1:7; Colossians 1:14,20; Revelation 1:5; Hebrews 1:3; Leviticus 17:11; 2 Chronicles 29:24; Hebrews 10:11-12; Hebrews 7:27; Romans 3:25; Romans 5:9). Amen.

Now let us unpack some of these points from Holy Writ concerning our Salvation. We read: "For I delivered unto you first of all that which I also received, how that Christ died for our sins according to the scriptures; And that he was buried, and that he rose again the third day according to the scriptures. (1 Corinthians 15:3-4) But he was wounded for our transgressions, he was bruised for our iniquities: the chastisement of our peace was upon him; and with his stripes we are healed. (Isaiah 53:5) And why are we healed with His stripes? We read: "For all have sinned, and come short of the glory of God; (Romans 3:23) For there is not a just man upon earth, that doeth good, and sinneth not. (Ecclesiastes 7:20). Therefore "your iniquities have separated between you and your God, and your sins have hid his face from you, that he will not hear. (Isaiah 59:2). Therefore "all things are of God, who hath reconciled us to himself by Jesus Christ, and hath given to us the ministry of reconciliation; To wit, that God was in Christ, reconciling the world unto himself, not imputing their trespasses unto them; and hath committed unto us the word of reconciliation. (2 Corinthians 5:18-19) For if when we were enemies, we were reconciled to God by the death of his Son, much more, being reconciled, we shall be saved by his life. (Rome 5:10)

Therefore, we must die through Christ Jesus our Lord through baptism. For "Know ye not, that so many of us as were baptized into Jesus Christ were baptized into his death? Therefore we are buried with him by baptism into death: that like as Christ was raised up from the dead by the glory of the Father, even so we also should walk in newness of life. For if we have been planted together in the likeness of his death, we shall be also in the likeness of his resurrection. Knowing this, that our old man is crucified with him, that the body of sin might be destroyed, that henceforth we should not serve sin. For he that is dead is freed from sin. Now if we be dead with Christ, we believe that we shall also live with him: (Romans 6:3-8) And the reason we must die through Christ through baptism, is so the penalty of sin which is death can be accomplished: "For the wages of sin is death; (Romans 6:23) For he that is dead is freed from sin. (Romans 6:7), therefore we die through Christ through baptism as we have read.

Now seeing that we die through the water of crucifixion which is baptism, we are then reborn, that is born again into a new creature (See 2 Corinthians 5:17; Galatians 6:15) and a new man (See Ephesians 4:24; Colossians 3:9-10; Ephesians 2:15), for the old man of sin was crucified through baptism and thusly died (See Romans 6:3-8). We read about the three interconnected methods of being born again (See John 3:3-7) being that we are born again by the water of baptism (See John 3:5; Acts 22:16; Acts 8:36; Acts 8:38; Acts 10:47), by receiving The Spirit of God (See John 3:5; Luke 11:13; Galatians 3:26) who will come to the Children of God, of which we are made a Child of God through faith in Christ Jesus our Lord (See Galatians 3:26), for we are born again through the Holy Scriptures (See 1 Peter 1:23-25; Compare John 3:5; Ephesians 5:26), for belief comes through reading The Holy Bible (See John 20:30-31; 1 John 5:13).

We read: "Jesus answered and said unto him, Verily, verily, I say unto thee, Except a man be born again, he cannot see the kingdom of God. Nicodemus saith unto him, How can a man be born when he is old? can he enter the second time into his mother's womb, and be born? Jesus answered, Verily, verily, I say unto thee, Except a man be born of water and of the Spirit, he cannot enter into the kingdom of God. That which is born of the flesh is flesh; and that which is born of the Spirit is spirit. Marvel not that I said unto thee, Ye must be born again. The wind bloweth where it listeth, and thou hearest the sound thereof; but canst not tell whence it cometh, and whither it goeth: so is every one that is born of the Spirit. (John 3:3-8).

Born Again by The Water: "Jesus answered, Verily, verily, I say unto thee, Except a man be born of water and of the Spirit, he cannot enter into the kingdom of God. (John 3:5) And as they went on their way, they came unto a certain water: and the eunuch said, See, here is water; what doeth hinder me to be baptized? (Acts 8:36; See Acts 8:38; Acts 10:47) And now why tarriest thou? arise, and be baptized, and wash away thy sins, calling on the name of the Lord. (Acts 22:16 See Revelation 1:5).

Born Again by The Spirit: "Jesus answered, Verily, verily, I say unto thee, Except a man be born of water and of the Spirit, he cannot enter into the kingdom of God. (John 3:5) If ye then, being evil, know how to give good gifts unto your children: how much more shall your heavenly Father give the Holy Spirit to them that ask him? (Luke 11:13) Then remembered I the word of the Lord, how that he said, John indeed baptized with water; but ye shall be baptized with the Holy Ghost. (Acts 11:16) And we are his witnesses of these things; and so is also the Holy Ghost, whom God hath given to them that obey him. (Acts 5:32) for "Not by works of righteousness which we have done, but according to his mercy he saved us, by the washing of regeneration, and renewing of the Holy Ghost; (Titus 3:5) Then Peter said unto them, Repent, and be baptized every one of you in the name of Jesus Christ for the remission of sins, and ye shall receive the gift of the Holy Ghost. (Acts 2:38) For ye are all the children of God by faith in Christ Jesus. For as many of you as have been baptized into Christ have put on Christ. (Galatians 3:26-27)

Born Again by The Holy Bible: "Being born again, not of corruptible seed, but of incorruptible, by the word of God, which liveth and abideth for ever. For all flesh is as grass, and all the glory of man as the flower of grass. The grass withereth, and the flower thereof falleth away: But the word of the Lord endureth for ever. And this is the word which by the gospel is preached unto you. (1 Peter 1:23-25) for "Of his own will begat he us with the word of truth, that we should be a kind of firstfruits of his creatures. (James 1:18) That he might sanctify and cleanse it with the washing of water by the word, (Ephesians 5:26)

Now consider more specifically the importance of reading and studying The Holy Words of God, The Bible if we are to be saved. We read that only those who eat the flesh of Christ Jesus our Lord will have eternal life (See John 6:53-56), which is clarified to be His Words (See John 6:63), these Words were given unto the Apostles (Compare John 14:26; John 16:13; John 15:26), therefore they are The Words of God (See 1 Thessalonians 2:13; 2 Corinthians 1:13; 1 John 4:6; 1 Corinthians 2:13; Ephesians 6:17), for Christ Jesus our Lord only ever spake The Words of God The Father (Compare Matthew 7:21; John 14:24), therefore we must read The Bible which is The Words of God to receive belief and thus be saved. We read: "For God so loved the world, that he gave his only begotten Son, that whosoever believeth in him should not perish, but have everlasting life. For God sent not his Son into the world to condemn the world; but that the world through him might be saved. He that believeth on him is not condemned: but he that believeth not is condemned already, because he hath not believed in the name of the only begotten Son of God. (John 3:16-18) And many other signs truly did Jesus in the presence of his disciples, which are not written in this book: But these are written, that ye might believe that Jesus is the Christ, the Son of God; and that believing ye might have life through his name. (John 20:30-31) These things have I written unto you that believe on the Son of God; that ye may know that ye have eternal life, and that ye may believe on the name of the Son of God. (1 John 5:13)

Now consider the other importance of belief which we receive through reading The Holy Words of God, The Bible, (See John 20:30-31; 1 John 5:13) is that by our belief in God, we are imputed with righteousness (See Romans 4:3-9,11,20-25), which is to be without sin (See Romans 4:3-8), which is important, for the unrighteous will not receive The Kingdom of God (See 1 Corinthians 6:9), and we are all unrighteous (See Romans 3:9-12,23), and we cannot make ourselves righteous (See Isaiah 59:2; Isaiah 64:6; Romans 3:9-12,23), therefore we believe in God, and then we are imputed with righteousness (See Romans 4:3-9,11,20-25) which is to be without sin (See Romans 4:3-8), and so being then righteous in the sight of God, we will be able to inherit The Kingdom of God and eternal life (Consider 1 Corinthians 6:9; Matthew 13:43; Matthew 25:34-37,46; Matthew 6:33; Compare 2 Corinthians 5:21; John 3:16-18; John 5:24; Romans 6:23; Romans 8:1), for if we confess our sins to God He will cleanse us from all unrighteousness (See 1 John 1:9), for Christ Jesus our Lord who is God (See John 20:28-29) is our mediator (See 1 Timothy 2:5), and so, we being in Christ Jesus our Lord through reading His Words we are made righteous through Him in totality (Compare 2 Corinthians 5:21; John 6:53-56,63; Ephesians 6:17), and so, we being now righteous in the sight of God through us being in Christ Jesus our Lord, we will be allowed into The Kingdom of God. Amen.

We read: "Know ye not that the unrighteous shall not inherit the kingdom of God? (1 Corinthians 6:9) As it is written, There is none righteous, no, not one: There is none that understandeth, there is none that seeketh after God. They are all gone out of the way, they are together become unprofitable; there is none that doeth good, no, not one. (Romans 3:10-12) Therefore Righteousness must be imputed unto us for us to be saved. We read: "For what saith the scriptures? Abraham believed God, and it was counted unto him for righteousness. Now to him that worketh is the reward not reckoned of grace, but of debt. But to him that worketh not, but believeth on him that justifieth the ungodly, his faith is counted for righteousness. Even as David also described the blessedness of the man, unto whom God imputed righteousness without works, Saying, Blessed are they whose iniquities are forgiven, and whose sins are covered. Blessed is the man to whom the Lord will not imputed sin. Commeth this blessedness then upon the circumcision only, or upon the uncircumcision also? for we say that faith was reckoned to Abraham for righteousness. (Romans 4:3-9) And he received the sign of circumcision, a seal of the righteousness of the faith which he had yet being uncircumcised: that he might be the father of all them that believe, though they be not circumcised; that righteousness might be imputed unto them also: (Romans 4:11) He staggered not at the promise of God through unbelief; but was strong in faith, giving glory to God; And being fully persuaded that, what he had promised, he was able also to perform. And therefore it was imputed to him for righteousness. Now it was not written for his sake alone, that it was imputed to him; But for us also, to whom it shall be imputed, if we believe on him that raised up Jesus our Lord from the dead; Who was delivered for our offenses, and raised again for our justification. (Romans 4:20-25).

Furthermore, we read that we are made righteous in Christ Jesus our Lord by being in Him through reading His Words. We read: "For he hath made him to be sin for us, who knew no sin; that we might be made the righteousness of God in him. (2 Corinthians 5:21) Then Jesus said unto them, Verily, verily, I say unto you, Except ye eat the flesh of the Son of man, and drink his blood, ye have no life in you. For my flesh is meat indeed, and my blood is drink indeed. He that eateth my flesh, and drinketh my blood, dwelleth in me, and I in him. (John 6:53-56) It is the spirit that quickeneth; the flesh profiteth nothing: the words that I speak unto you, they are spirit, and they are life. (John 6:63) And take the helmet of salvation, and the sword of the Spirit, which is the word of God. (Ephesians 6:17 See 1 John 4:6; 1 John 5:13; 1 Corinthians 2:13; 2 Corinthians 1:13; John 20:30-31; John 10:27-28; Acts 13:27)

Now let us consider exactly how our atonement is made through the death of Christ Jesus our Lord upon The Cross that redeems and reconciles us unto redemption to God through His Blood. We read that the sacrifices in The Old Testament were but a shadow of the true atonement offering of The Lamb of God, Christ Jesus our Lord, who is our Passover Sacrifice in who's blood cleanseth us and washes us from our sins. We read: "But if we walk in the light, as he is in the light, we have fellowship one with another, and the blood of Jesus Christ his Son cleanseth us from all sin. (1 John 1:7) Forasmuch as ye know that ye are not redeemed with corruptible things, as silver and gold, from your vain conversation received by tradition from your fathers; But with the precious blood of Christ, as a lamb without blemish and without spot: (1 Peter 1:18-19) Purge out therefore the old leaven, that ye may be a new lump, as ye are unleavened. For even Christ our passover is sacrificed for us: (1 Corinthians 5:7) For the life of the flesh is in the blood: and I have given it to you upon the alter to make an atonement for your souls: for it is the blood that maketh an atonement for the soul. (Leviticus 17:11) And the priest killed them, and they made reconciliation with their blood upon the alter, to make an atonement for all Israel: for the king commanded that the burnt offering and the sin offering should be made for all Israel. (2 Chronicles 29:24) And looking upon Jesus as he walked, he saith, Behold the Lamb of God! (John 1:36; See John 1:29)

For the law having a shadow of good things to come, and not the very image of the things, can never with those sacrifices which they offered year by year continually make the comers thereunto perfect. For then would they not have ceased to be offered? because that the worshipers once purged should have had no more conscience of sins. But in those sacrifices there is a remembrance again made of sins every year. For it is not possible that the blood of bulls and of goats should take away sins. Whereunto when he cometh into the world, he saith, Sacrifices and offering thou wouldest not, but a body hast thou prepared me: (Hebrews 10:1-5) By the which will we are sanctified through the offering of the body of Jesus Christ once for all. And every priest standeth daily ministering and offering oftentimes the same sacrifices, which can never take away sins: But this man, after he had offered one sacrifice for sins for ever, sat down at the right hand of God; From henceforth expecting till his enemies be made his footstool. For by one offering he hath perfected for ever them that are sanctified. (Hebrews 10:10-14) Who needeth not daily, as those high priests, to offer up sacrifice, first for his own sins, and then for the people's: for this he did once, when he offered up himself. (Hebrews 7:27) And almost all things are by the law purged with blood; and without shedding of blood is no remission. (Hebrews 9:22)

Therefore "I delivered unto you first of all that which I also received, how that Christ died for our sins according to the scriptures; And that he was buried, and that he rose again the third day according to the scriptures: (1 Corinthians 15:3-4) For he hath made him to be sin for us, who knew no sin; that we might be made the righteousness of God in him. (2 Corinthians 5:21 See John 6:53-56,63) For the bodies of those beasts, whose blood is brought into the sanctuary by the high priest for sin, are burnet without the camp. Wherefore Jesus also, that he might sanctify the people with his own blood, suffered without the gate. (Hebrews 13:11-12) Neither by the blood of goats and calves, but by his own blood he entered in once into the holy place, having obtained eternal redemption for us. (Hebrews 9:12)

Wherefore, holy brethren, partakers of the heavenly calling, consider the Apostle and High Priest of our profession, Christ Jesus; (Hebrews 3:1)) In whom we have redemption through his blood, the forgiveness of sins, according to the riches of his grace; (Ephesians 1:7) In whom we have redemption through his blood, even the forgiveness of sins: (Colossians 1:14) And, having made peace through the blood of his cross, by him to reconcile all things unto himself; by him, I say, whether they be things in earth, or things in heaven. (Colossians 1:20) For He "washed us from our sins in his own blood, (Revelation 1:5 See Acts 22:16; Psalm 51:2) And they sung a new song, saying, Thou art worthy to take the book, and to open the seals thereof: for thou wast slain, and hast redeemed us to God by thy blood out of every kindred, and tongue, and people, and nation; (Revelation 5:9) Much more then, being now justified by his blood, we shall be saved from wrath through him. (Romans 5:9) Whom God hath set forth to be a propitiation through faith in his blood, to declare, I say, at this time his righteousness: that he might be just, and the justifier of him which believe in Jesus. (Romans 3:25-26) By the which will we are sanctified through the offering of the body of Jesus Christ once for all. (Hebrews 10:10) Who was delivered for our offenses, and raised again for our justification. (Romans 4:25). Amen.

More Texts: (Romans 5:1-3; Romans 3:24; Romans 5:9; 1 Corinthians 6:11; Titus 3:7; Acts 2:38; Acts 3:19).

WHAT IT MEANS TO LIVE A CHRISTIAN LIFE

Pure religion and undefiled before God and the Father is this, To visit the fatherless and the widows in their affliction, and to keep himself unspotted from the world. (James 1:27) For bodily exercise profiteth little: but godliness is profitable unto all things, having promise of the life that now is, and of that which is to come. (1 Timothy 4:8) For it is written, As I live saith the Lord, every knee shall bow to me, and every tongue shall confess to God. So then every one of us shall give account of himself to God. (Romans 14:11-12) Therefore now, seeing as we shall indeed have to answer for all things that we have done in our bodies, words, and thoughts on that Day of Judgment before God, let us consider Godliness, let us consider Righteousness, let us consider how we can be kept unspotted from the world so that we can stand unashamed before God on that day.

We see as our example of righteousness that we should follow, our Lord Jesus Christ (See 1 John 2:6; 1 Peter 2:21), and it is through His Word, The Word of God, that we learn instruction in righteousness that we might be perfect (See 2 Timothy 3:16-17), which indeed brings us to His Word, The Holy Bible. For there are three main duties that we as Christians personally have in this life, as Scripture shows unto us, and they are: First: Our Duty To God, Second: Our Duty To Our fellowman, Third: Our Duty To Ourselves. These three duties are inseparable from each other and linked together for the simple reason that we find them in Holy Writ as a complete whole, which means, for us to be truly whole as Christians we must have them all within us, that is, we must fulfill them each and all. Therefore now, let us discuss each of these categories that we have mentioned, and discover that which Holy Writ reveals unto us about these three duties that we must perform as followers of Christ Jesus our Lord.

The Three Duties Of Every Christian

Our Lord Jesus Christ hath said: "He that is not with me is against me; and he that gathereth not with me scattereth abroad. (Matthew 12:30) Therefore "I am crucified with Christ: nevertheless I live: yet not I, but Christ liveth in me: and the life which I now live in the flesh I live by the faith of the Son of God, who loved me, and gave himself for me. (Galatians 2:20) saith Paul under inspiration. For "If any man will come after me, let him deny himself, and take up his cross daily, and follow me. (Luke 9:23) For "He that loveth his life shall lose it: and he that hateth his life in this world shall keep it unto life eternal. (John 12:25) saith our Lord Jesus Christ.

Which brings us fully into our discussion in this chapter, for, we must indeed learn how it is that we as Christians must order and live our lives. For as we read: "But seek ye first the kingdom of God, and his righteousness; and all these things shall be added unto you. Take therefore no thought for the morrow: for the morrow shall take thought for the things of itself. Sufficient unto the day is the evil thereof. (Matthew 6:33-34) If ye then be risen with Christ, seek those things which are above, where Christ sitteth on the right hand of God. (Colossians 3:1) For where your treasure is, there will your heart be also, (Matthew 6:21) Set your affections on things above, not on things on the earth. (Colossians 3:2) For we brought nothing into this world, and it is certain we can carry nothing out. And having food and raiment let us be therewith content. (1 Timothy 6:7-8)

And how can we do this? How can we truly set our affections on the heavenly things of God? We read: I beseech you therefore, brethren, by the mercies of God, that ye present your bodies a living sacrifice, holy, acceptable unto God, which is your reasonable service. And be not conformed to this world: but be ye transformed by the renewing of your mind, that ye may prove what is that good, and acceptable, and perfect, will of God. (Romans 12:1-2) by "Casting down imaginations, and every high thing that exalteth itself against the knowledge of God, and bringing into captivity every thought to the obedience of Christ; (2 Corinthians 10:5) Whether therefore ye eat, or drink, or whatsoever ye do, do all to the glory of God. (1 Corinthians 10:31) For "they that are Christ's have crucified the flesh with the affections and lusts. (Galatians 5:24 See 1 Peter 1:22; John 17:17)

Which brings us very naturally to our first great duty towards God, ourselves, and others, which concerns our personal behavior of what we look at and behold with our eyes, for what we look at, we will inevitably think about, and what we think about is who we really are as we read: "For as he thinketh in his heart, so is he: (Proverbs 23:7), which is a why it is so very important to follow the command that states: "Let the wicked forsake his way, and the unrighteous man his thoughts: and let him return unto the LORD, and he will have mercy upon him; and to our God, for he will abundantly pardon. (Isaiah 55:7). Which of course is a problem, for "The heart is deceitful above all things, and desperately wicked: who can know it? (Jeremiah 17:9), and, "There is a way which seemeth right unto a man, but the end thereof are the ways of death. (Proverbs 14:12)

Therefore what ought we to do? We read: "Trust in the LORD with all thine heart; and lean not unto thine own understanding. In all thy ways acknowledge him, and he shall direct thy paths. (Proverbs 3:5-6) Submit yourselves therefore to God. Resist the devil, and he will flee from you. Draw nigh to God, and he will draw nigh to you. Cleanse your hands, ye sinners; and purify your hearts, ye double minded. Be afflicted, and mourn, and weep: let your laughter be turned to mourning, and your joy to heaviness. Humble yourselves in the sight of the Lord, and he shall lift you up. (James 4:7-10)

And so, how can we forsake our evil thoughts and be clean? We must with all diligence guard the avenues of our minds by following the inspired words of David where he declares: "I will set no wicked thing before mine eyes: I hate the work of them that turn aside; it shall not cleave to me. (Psalm 101:3) For "The night is far spent, the day is at hand: let us therefore cast off the works of darkness, and let us put on the armour of light. (Romans 13:12) For we are to "have no fellowship with the unfruitful works of darkness, but rather reprove them. (Ephesians 5:11), for "If we say that we have fellowship with him, and walk in darkness, we lie, and do not the truth: (1 John 1:6). Therefore, we pray that God: "Turn away mine eyes from beholding vanity; and quicken thou me in the way. (Psalm 119:37), for again, our Lord and Savior Jesus Christ protest most sternly that "He that is not with me is against me; and he that gathereth not with me scattereth abroad. (Matthew 12:30), therefore we must guard the avenues of our minds by not watching and beholding filthy and sinful behavior in any form in this life, that is, not by personal associations, nor from television, or video games, or movies, and not even in music or idol conversation, for "Woe unto them that call evil good, and good evil; that put darkness for light, and light for darkness; that put bitter for sweet, and sweet for bitter! (Isaiah 5:20) For as he thinketh in his heart, so is he: (Proverbs 23:7), therefore "let every one that nameth the name of Christ depart from iniquity. (2 Timothy 2:19) For whether we live, we live unto the Lord; and whether we die, we die unto the Lord: whether we live therefore, or die, we are the Lord's. (Romans 14:8)

And so, how can we fully mentally depart from iniquity? We read: "Finally, brethren, whatsoever things are true, whatsoever things are honest, whatsoever things are just, whatsoever things are pure, whatsoever things are lovely, whatsoever things are of good report; if there be any virtue, and if there be any praise, think on these things. (Philippians 4:8). For we must indeed be "Casting down imaginations, and every high thing that exalteth itself against the knowledge of God, and bringing into captivity every thought to the obedience of Christ; (2 Corinthians 10:5) Yea, doubtless, and I count all things but loss for the excellency of the knowledge of Christ Jesus my Lord: for whom I suffer the loss of all things, and do count them but dung, that I may win Christ, (Philippians 3:8)

Therefore we must set aside all violet things that we may behold (See Psalm 11:5), and lustful things as well (See Matthew 5:28; 2 Peter 2:8), for as we read: "Love not the world, neither the things that are in the world. If any man love the world, the love of the Father is not in him. For all that is in the world, the lust of the flesh, and the lust of the eyes, and the pride of life, is not of the Father, but is of the world. And the world passeth away, and the lust thereof: but he that doeth the will of God abideth for ever. (1 John 2:15-17) Therefore "Blessed is the man that endureth temptation: for when he is tried, he shall receive the crown of life, which the Lord hath promised to them that love him. Let no man say when he is tempted, I am tempted of God: for God cannot be tempted with evil, neither tempteth he any man: But every man is tempted, when he is drawn away of his own lust, and enticed. Then when lust hath conceived, it bringeth forth sin: and sin, when it is finished, bringeth forth death. Do no err, my beloved brethren. Every good gift and every perfect gift is from above, and cometh down from the Father of lights, with whom is no variableness, neither shadow of turning. (James 1:12-17)

Therefore fulfill that which was written for our learning (See Romans 15:4; 2 Timothy 3:16-17) that states: "I will set no wicked thing before mine eyes: I hate the work of them that turn aside; it shall not cleave to me. (Psalm 101:3) For as he thinketh in his heart, so is he: (Proverbs 23:7) For "Ye adulterers and adulteresses, know ye not that the friendship of the world is enmity with God? whosoever therefore will be a friend of the world is the enemy of God. (James 4:4) For let us not be as the wicked "Who knowing the judgments of God, that they who commit such things are worthy of death, not only do the same, but have pleasure in them that do them. (Romans 1:23 See 1 Corinthians 13:6; Ephesians 5:11; Isaiah 5:20; Proverbs 17:15; Proverbs 29:27; 1 Peter 4:4; 1 Peter 4:16; 2 Timothy 3:12).

Now it will be rightly asked: How can we determine that which is truly within our heart, seeing that what we think reveals who we really are? (See Proverbs 23:7) We learn that what we utter with our tongue, that is, our words that we speak is the great revealer of who we really are. We read: "A good man out of the good treasures of his heart bringeth forth that which is good; and an evil man out of the evil treasure of his heart bringeth forth that which is evil: for of the abundance of the heart his mouth speaketh. (Luke 6:45) For from within, out of the heart of men, proceed evil thoughts, adulteries, fornications, murders, Thefts, covetousness, wickedness, deceit, lasciviousness, an evil eye, blasphemy, pride, foolishness: All these evil things come from within, and defile the man. (Mark 7:21-23 See Romans 10:9-10; Matthew 10:32-33) Therefore "Be not deceived: evil communication corrupt good manners. (1 Corinthians 15:33 See 1 Peter 1:13-16; 1 Peter 2:1-3,11-12,21-24; 1 Peter 3:8-18), and this communication that corrupts us, is not just what we ourselves say, but the evil communication of others will corrupt us as well, therefore, just as we must guard the avenues of our mind by what we look at, we must also guard against what we say and what we hear others utter through their mouth, for we must avoid the filthy communication and bad language from ourselves and others. For in this way, our prayer of asking God to makes us clean will not be hindered by our own sinful actions. Therefore: "Create in me a clean heart, O God; and renew a right spirit within me. (Psalm 51:10 See Isaiah 1:18)

This brings us to our next point of discussion that we must Trust God without hesitation, while mistrusting others and ourselves. We read: "Pride goeth before destruction, and a haughty spirit before a fall. (Proverbs 16:18) Therefore "Humble yourselves in the sight of the Lord, and he shall lift you up. (James 4:10) For "There is a way which seemeth right unto a man, but the end thereof are the ways of death. (Proverbs 14:12) For "The heart is deceitful above all things, and desperately wicked: who can know it? (Jeremiah 17:9) Therefore "Trust in the LORD with all thine heart; and lean not unto thine own understanding. In all thy ways acknowledge him, and he shall direct thy paths. (Proverbs 3:5-6) For "Thou wilt keep him in perfect peace, whose mind is stayed on thee: because he trusteth in thee. (Isaiah 26:3) For "Thus saith the LORD; Cursed be the man that trusteth in man, and maketh flesh his arm, and whose heart departeth from the LORD. (Jeremiah 17:5), but "Blessed is the man that trusteth in the LORD, and whose hope the LORD is. (Jeremiah 17:7) For "We ought to obey God rather than men. (Acts 5:29) Therefore "Take ye heed every one of his neighbour, and trust ye not in any brother: for every brother will utterly supplant, and every neighbour will walk with slanders. (Jeremiah 9:4) Trust ye not in a friend, put ye not confidence in a guide: keep the doors of thy mouth from her that lieth in thy bosom. (Micah 7:5)

Now, even though we are to never trust anyone, especially concerning the things of God, of which we can trust nothing but The Holy Bible itself, (See Romans 15:4; 2 Timothy 3:16-17), this does not mean we can stop loving our fellowman and doing that which is good, for "If a man say, I love God, and hateth his brother, he is a liar: for he that loveth not his brother whom he hath seen, how can he love God whom he hath not seen? (1 John 4:20) for "Therewith bless we God, even the Father; and therewith curse we men, which are made after the similitude of God. Out of the same mouth proceedeth blessing and cursing. My brethren, these things ought not to be. (James 3:9-10).

Now consider some of the other points in loving our fellowman. We read: "If ye fulfil the royal law according to the scriptures, Thou shalt love thy neighbour as thyself, ye do well. (James 2:8) Therefore all things whatsoever ye would that men should do to you, do ye even so to them: for this is the law and the prophets. (Matthew 7:12) For "Let him know, that he which converteth the sinner from the error of his way shall save a soul from death, and shall hide a multitude of sins. (James 5:20) Go ye therefore, and teach all nations, baptizing them in the name of the Father, and of the Son, and of the Holy Ghost: Teaching them to observe all things whatsoever I have commanded you: and, lo, I am with you always, even unto the end of the world. Amen. (Matthew 28:19-20) For "What doth it profit, my brethren, though a man say he hath faith, and have not works? can faith save him? If a brother or sister be naked, and destitute of daily food, And one of you say unto them, Depart in peace, be ye warmed and filled; notwithstanding ye give them not those things which are needful to the body; what doth in prophet? (James 2:14-16) Therefore "Let your light so shine before men, that they may see your good works, and glorify your Father in heaven. (Matthew 5:16 See Matthew 25:31-46; Matthew 6:3). Furthermore, we learn that we must forgive men all the sins and evils that they have done unto us so that God Himself will forgive us. "For he shall have judgment without mercy, that hath shewed no mercy; and mercy rejoiceth against judgment. (James 2:13) For if ye forgive men their trespasses, your heavenly Father will also forgive you: But if ye forgive not men their trespasses, neither will your heavenly Father forgive your trespasses. (Matthew 6:14-15).

And now, seeing we have discussed some of the important points of our personal behavior, and how we should minister towards others as Holy Writ reveals unto us, let us now turn to the more weightier matters of our personal duty towards God Himself. "For whether we live, we live unto the Lord; and whether we die, we die unto the Lord: whether we live therefore, or die, we are the Lord's. (Romans 14:8) For "In all thy ways acknowledge him, and he shall direct thy paths. (Proverbs 3:6) for he hath said, I will never leave thee, nor forsake thee. (Hebrews 13:5) And so, we must consider the necessity of prayer, studying and reading The Holy Bible, confessing our faith in Christ Jesus our Lord unto the very end, and actually having personal belief and faith in God.

We read: "For God so loved the world, that he gave his only begotten Son, that whosoever believeth in him should not perish, but have everlasting life. For God sent not his Son into the world to condemn the world; but that the world through him might be saved. He that believeth on him is not condemned: but he that believeth not is condemned already, because he hath not believed in the name of the only begotten Son of God. (John 3:16-18) For "He that is not with me is against me; and he that gathereth not with me scattereth abroad. (Matthew 12:30) Therefore "Whosoever therefore will confess me before men, him will I confess also before my Father which is in heaven. But whosoever shall deny me before men, him will I also deny before my Father which is in heaven. (Matthew 10:32-33) For "I say unto you, That every idle word that men shall speak, they shall give account thereof in the day of judgment. For by thy words thou shalt be justified, and by thy words thou shalt be condemned. (Matthew 12:36-37) For "To him give all the prophets witness, that through his name whosoever believeth in him shall receive remission of sins. (Acts 10:43) Then said they unto him, What shall we do, that we might work the works of God? Jesus answered and said unto them, This is the work of God, that ye believe on him whom he hath sent. (John 6:28-29)

And how do we gain belief in Christ Jesus our Lord? We learn that it is through reading The Holy Bible: "And many other signs truly did Jesus in the presence of his disciples, which are not written in this book: But these are written, that ye might believe that Jesus is the Christ, the Son of God; and that believing ye might have life through his name. (John 20:30-31) These things have I written unto you that believe on the Son of God; that ye may know that ye have eternal life, and that ye may believe on the name of the Son of God. (1 John 5:13) For saith our Lord Jesus Christ "Verily, verily, I say unto you, He that heareth my word, and believeth on him that sent me, hath everlasting life, and shall not come into condemnation; but is passed from death unto life. (John 5:24 See Romans 8:1; Romans 10:8-17) For "My sheep hear my voice, and I know them, and they follow me: And I give unto them eternal life; and they shall never perish, neither shall any man pluck them out of my hand. (John 10:27-28)

Then Jesus said unto them, Verily, verily, I say unto you, Except ye eat the flesh of the Son of man, and drink his blood, ye have no life in you. (John 6:53-54) It is the spirit that quickeneth; the flesh profiteth nothing: the words that I speak unto you, they are spirit, and they are life. (John 6:63) Therefore "take the helmet of salvation, and the sword of the Spirit which is the word of God: (Ephesians 6:17), so that ye may "Study to shew thyself approved unto God, a workman that needeth not to be ashamed, rightly dividing the word of truth. (2 Timothy 2:15) For whatsoever things were written aforetime were written for our learning, that we through patience and comfort of the scriptures might have hope. (Romans 15:4) For "All scripture is given by inspiration of God, and is profitable for doctrine, for reproof, for correction, for instruction in righteousness: That the man of God may be perfect, thoroughly furnished unto all good works. (2 Timothy 3:16-17) For ye are all the children of God by faith in Christ Jesus. For as many of you as have been baptized into Christ have put on Christ. (Galatians 3:26-27 See Mark 16:15-16)

And now we read on the importance of prayer to God that we must "Be careful for nothing; but in every thing by prayer and supplication with thanksgiving let your requests be made known to God. (Philippians 4:6) for he hath said, I will never leave thee, nor forsake thee. (Hebrews 13:5) For "all things, whatsoever ye shall ask in prayer, believing, ye shall receive. (Matthew 21:22 See John 16:24) except for the following: "Ye ask, and receive not, because ye ask amiss, that ye may consume it upon your lusts. (James 4:3) Therefore "seek ye first the kingdom of God, and his righteousness; and all these things shall be added unto you. (Matthew 6:33). Amen.

More Texts: (Jeremiah 17:9-10; Psalm 51:10; Isaiah 1:18; Matthew 5:48; 1 Corinthians 2:9; Jeremiah 29:11 See 2 Timothy 3:16-17; Romans 15:4; Psalm 37:25; Luke 6:26; Romans 14:10; Luke 21:36; Matthew 12:36; Titus 2:8; 1 Timothy 6:3-4; 1 Peter 3:9; Matthew 5:39; Luke 6:35; Ephesians 6:12; 1 Peter 2:21-23; 1 John 3:6; 1 Peter 2:23; 1 Timothy 5:8; 1 Timothy 2:9-10; 1 Timothy 6:6-12; James 4:10; Ephesians 6:12-13; 2 Timothy 2:19; Titus 2:1-4; Titus 3:1-11,14; Titus 3:5.8,14; 1 Timothy 6:7-8; Hebrews 13:5; Romans 8:31; Matthew 5:39-48; Matthew 6:1; Titus 1:15-16; Titus 1:3; Romans 1:17; Romans 1:17; Proverbs 14:12; Proverbs 3:5-7; Isaiah 26:3; Hebrews 13:5; Psalm 59:16; Acts 5:29; 2 Timothy 3:12; Jeremiah 17:5-8; Jeremiah 9:4; Micah 7:5; Luke 11:4; Matthew 6:14-15; Matthew 5:43-45; Matthew 12:30; Matthew 10:32-33; John 6:28-29; John 3:16-18; Hosea 4:1-3; Hosea 4:6; 2 Timothy 3:16-17; Hosea 10:12-14; Hosea 14:9; Romans 15:4; Ecclesiastes 1:9; Isaiah 55:6; Hebrews 13:5; James 1:27; James 1:2-8; James 1:9-11; James 1:2-4; James 1:12-18; James 2:1-9; James 3:5-6; James 3:10-11; James 3:13-16; James 4:7-10; James 4:3; James 4:15-17; James 5:8-9;

James 5:20; 1 Peter 4:3-4; John 15:19; 2 Timothy 3:12; 1 Corinthians 13:1-3; 1 Peter 4:8; 1 Corinthians 13:4-5; 1 Peter 5:6-10; 2 Timothy 3:12; Psalm 34:13; Ephesians 4:31; 1 Peter 2:1; 1 Peter 4:4; Hebrews 12:5-8; Hebrews 13:5; 1 Peter 5:7; Isaiah 26:3; John 13:34-35; 1 John 4:10; 1 Corinthians 2:9; 1 John 4:12,20; 3 John 11; Romans 8:35-37; 1 John 4:11-12; Proverbs 14:34; Proverbs 14:22; Jeremiah 29:11-13; Isaiah 29:11-13; 1 Corinthians 1:25; Matthew 22:37-39; Psalm 73:25-26)

UNDERSTANDING THE HOLY TRINITY

We come now to what is perhaps one of the most misunderstood doctrines of Christianity, and it is this way, because it concerns God Himself (Consider John 3:12), that is The Holy Trinity, that is, JEHOVAH our God (See Isaiah 37:16; Isaiah 45:18) being One God (See Deuteronomy 6:4; James 2:19), yet being completely separate into three individual personages (See Matthew 28:19; Genesis 11:7,5-11; Genesis 1:26; Isaiah 6:8), yet truly One (Isaiah 43:10; Compare Ephesians 4:5; Matthew 28:19; Acts 2:38; Zechariah 14:9) at the same time. We read: "For there are three that bear record in heaven, the Father, the Word, and the Holy Ghost: and these three are one. (1 John 5:7)

Now despite this very clear declaration from Holy Writ, there is still contention from some on this doctrine. Yet consider. Holy Scripture makes it very clear that our God is JEHOVAH (See Isaiah 37:16; Isaiah 45:18; Exodus 6:3), and that no one has the name JEHOVAH except JEHOVAH (See Psalm 83:18), and that there is no God before or after JEHOVAH (See Isaiah 43:10), which is important, for we see declared in Holy Writ that God The Father, is JEHOVAH (Compare Romans 10:9; Acts 5:30; Acts 7:32; Exodus 6:3; Galatians 1:1) and God (See Ephesians 1:3; 2 John 3), that God The Son our Lord Jesus Christ is JEHOVAH (Compare Isaiah 40:3; Matthew 3:1-3; John 1:19-23; John 3:27-28) and God (See John 20:28-29), and that God The Most Holy Ghost is JEHOVAH (Compare Genesis 2:7; Job 33:4) and God (See Acts 5:3-4), we thus see declared through Holy Writ, that our One God JEHOVAH is God The Father, who is The Father of our Lord and Savior Jesus Christ, and God The Son, our Lord and Savior Jesus Christ Himself, and God The Most Holy Spirit, and these Three (See Genesis 11:7,5-11) are truly One (See Isaiah 43:10) in totality (Compare Ephesians 4:5; Matthew 28:19; Acts 2:38; Zechariah 14:9).

Now let us unpack each of these points, but before we do it should be pointed out that most of the places that The Old Testament has The Word LORD in all capital letters, this is actually The Name of our Great God JEHOVAH that was translated as LORD in The Bible. Therefore, in this chapter, we will place The Name JEHOVAH next to LORD when we give a quote from Holy Writ that contains LORD, that is, JEHOVAH in the text.

A: Now consider that our God is JEHOVAH. We read: "And I appeared unto Abraham, unto Isaac, and unto Jacob, by the name of God Almighty, but by my name JEHOVAH was I not known to them. (Exodus 6:3) O LORD (JEHOVAH) of hosts, God of Israel that dwellest between the cherubims, thou art the God, even thou alone, of all the kingdoms of the earth: thou hast made heaven and earth. (Isaiah 37:16) For thus saith the LORD (JEHOVAH) that created the heavens; God himself that formed the earth and made it; he hath established it, he created it not in vain, he formed it to be inhabited: I am the LORD; (JEHOVAH) and there is none else. (Isaiah 45:18) I am the LORD, (JEHOVAH) and there is none else, there is no God beside me: I girded thee, though thou hast not known me: (Isaiah 45:5) Now therefore, O LORD (JEHOVAH) our God, save us from his hand, that all the kingdoms of the earth may know that thou art the LORD, (JEHOVAH) even thou only. (Isaiah 37:20)

B: No one has the Name JEHOVAH but JEHOVAH. We read: "That men may know that thou, whose name alone is JEHOVAH, art the most high over all the earth. (Psalm 83:18)

C: There was no God before or after JEHOVAH. We read: "Ye are my witnesses, saith the LORD, (JEHOVAH) and my servant whom I have chosen: that ye may know and believe me, and understand that I am he: before me there was no God formed, neither shall there be after me. (Isaiah 43:10)

D: JEHOVAH is One God. We read: "Here, O Israel: The LORD (JEHOVAH) our God is one LORD: (JEHOVAH) (Deuteronomy 6:4)

E: We see that JEHOVAH has a separate distinctness, notice "Us" in the text. We read: "Go to, let us go down, and there confound their language, that they may not understand one another's speech. (Genesis 11:7) Therefore is the name of it called Babel; because the LORD (JEHOVAH) did there confound the language of all the earth: (Genesis 11:9 See Genesis 11:5-9)

F: We see that JEHOVAH is truly Three yet One. We read in comparison: "One Lord, one faith, one baptism, (Ephesians 4:5) Go ye therefore, and teach all nations, baptizing them in the name of the Father, and of the Son, and of the Holy Ghost: (Matthew 28:19) Then Peter said unto them, Repent, and be baptized every one of you in the name of Jesus Christ for the remission of sins, and ye shall receive the gift of the Holy Ghost." (Acts 2:38) And the LORD (JEHOVAH) shall be king over all the earth: in that day shall there be one LORD, (JEHOVAH) and his name one. (Zechariah 14:9)

G: God The Father is God: "Grace be with you, mercy, and peace, from God the Father, and from the Lord Jesus Christ, the Son of the Father, in truth and love. (2 John 3) Blessed be the God and Father of our Lord Jesus Christ, which according to his abundant mercy hath begotten us again unto a lively hope by the resurrection of Jesus Christ from the dead, (1 Peter 1:3)

H: God The Father is JEHOVAH: "That if thou shalt confess with thy mouth the Lord Jesus and shalt believe in thine heart that God hath raised him from the dead, thou shalt be saved. (Romans 10:9) The God of our fathers raised up Jesus, whom ye slew and hanged on a tree. (Acts 5:30) The God of Abraham, and of Isaac, and of Jacob, the God of our fathers, hath glorified his Son Jesus; whom ye delivered up, and denied him in the presents of Pilate, when he was determined to let him go. (Acts 3:13) Saying, I am the God of thy fathers, the God of Abraham, and the God of Isaac, and the God of Jacob. Then Moses trembled, and durst not behold. (Acts 7:32) And I appeared unto Abraham, unto Isaac, and unto Jacob, by the name of God Almighty, but by my name JEHOVAH was I not known to them. (Exodus 6:3) Paul, an apostle (not of men, neither by man, but by Jesus Christ, and God the Father, who raised him from the dead;) (Galatians 1:1) Therefore we are buried with him by baptism into death: that like as Christ was raised up from the dead by the glory of the Father, even so we also should walk in newness of life. (Romans 6:4)

I: God The Son is God: "And Thomas answered and said unto him, My LORD and my God. Jesus saith unto him, Thomas, because thou hast seen me, thou hast believed: blessed are they that have not seen, and yet have believed. (John 20:28-29)

J: God The Son is JEHOVAH: "The voice of him that crieth in the wilderness, Prepare ye the way of the LORD, (JEHOVAH) make straight in the desert a highway for our God. (Isaiah 40:3) In those days came John the Baptist, preaching in the wilderness of Judea, And saying, Repent, ye: for the kingdom of heaven is at hand. For this is he that was spoken of by the prophet Esaias, saying, The voice of one crying in the wilderness, Prepare ye the way of the Lord, make his paths straight. (Matthew 3:1-3) And this is the record of John, when the Jews sent priests and Levites from Jerusalem to ask him, Who art thou? And he confessed, and denied not; but confessed, I am not the Christ. And they asked him, What then? Art thou Elias? And he said, I am not. Art thou that prophet? And he answered, No. Then said they unto him, Who art thou? that we may give an answer to them that sent us. What sayest thou of thyself? He said, I am the voice of one crying in the wilderness, Make straight the way of the Lord, as said the prophet Esaias. (John 1:19-23) John answered and said, A man can receive nothing, except it be given him from heaven. Ye yourselves bear me witness, that I said, I am not the Christ, but that I am sent before him. (John 3:27-28)

K: God The Most Holy Ghost is God: "But Peter said Ananias, why hath Satan filled thine heart to lie to the Holy Ghost, and keep back part of the price of the land? Whiles it remained, was it not thine own? and after it was sold, was it not in thine own power? why hast thou conceived this thing in thine heart? thou hast not lied unto men, but unto God. (Acts 5:3-4)

L: God The Most Holy Ghost is JEHOVAH: "And the LORD (JEHOVAH) God formed man of the dust of the ground, and breathed into his nostrils the breath of life; and man became a living soul. (Genesis 2:7) The spirit of God hath made me, and the breath of the Almighty hath given me life. (Job 33:4)

M: Thus as we have see from Holy Writ alone our One God truly is The Holy Trinity. Amen.

BIBLE PROPHECY AND CHRISTIANITY

For unto us a child is born, unto us a son is given: and the government shall be upon his shoulder: and his name shall be called Wonderful, Counsellor, The mighty God, The everlasting Father, The Prince of Peace. (Isaiah 9:6) But he was wounded for our transgressions, he was bruised for our iniquities: the chastisement of our peace was upon him; and with his stripes we are healed. (Isaiah 53:5) These two passages from The Old Testament are but two of many that pointed to our Lord and Savior Jesus Christ as the prophesied Messiah that was to come, that we see fully fulfilled by Him in The New Testament. Now while these two declarations from The Old Testament maybe the most famous and well quoted concerning our Lord and Savior Jesus Christ, there is however the prophecy that foretold the exact time when He was to arrive, which is contained in the prophecy of Daniel 9:25 that was written 151 years before it happened and happened in history exactly as The Bible stated that it would, and this according to the date of the oldest portion of the Dead Sea Scrolls of The Book of Daniel (Around 125 B.C.).

We read: "Know therefore and understand, that from the going forth of the commandment to restore and to build Jerusalem unto the Messiah the Prince shall be seven weeks, and threescore and two weeks: the street shall be built again, and the wall even in troublous times. (Daniel 9:25)

The word translated as "weeks" here in the text, is translated from the Hebrew word "Shabua" that can either stand for a period denoting "days of 7" or "years of 7", the context of what is written determines which, and in this prophecy of Daniel that we have just read, the "weeks" refer to "years of 7", for two simple reasons. First: Daniel, when he receives this prophecy is considering another prophecy that concerns "years" (See Daniel 9:2)

Second: When Daniel uses "Shabua" in another places, he specifically mentions that it denotes "weeks of days", as we can read in the margin of Daniel 10:2-3 in the King James Version, (See Daniel 10:2-3 in the Geneva Version, and Young's Literal Translation), thus showing us that when Daniel does not qualify the meaning of "Shabua" translated as "weeks", that this denotes "years", for when he does qualify "Shabua" he specifically states that it is for days.

This means, that in the prophecy of Daniel 9:25, we know that The Messiah is to arrive 483 years (69 weeks of years) from the going forth of the commandment to build and restore Jerusalem. Note: We see in prophecy that days denote years (See Numbers 14:34; Ezekiel 4:6; Luke 13:32).

We learn form Scripture, that the command to build and restore Jerusalem was given in the first day, of the first month, of the seventh year of king Artaxerxes (See Ezra 7:6-10; Ezra 9:9), that is 457 B.C. For since the laws of the Medes and Persians cannot be changed (See Daniel 6:8,12,15; Esther 1:19), and we see that king Cyrus had previously issuing a decree to build Jerusalem (See 2 Chronicles 36:23; Isaiah 44:28; Isaiah 45:1,13; Ezra 6:14; Ezra 9:9; Zechariah 1:16), this means that when the decree to restore Jerusalem to the Laws of God took place in 457 B.C. by king Artaxerxes (See Ezra 7:25-26; Isaiah 1:26), this means the command to build and restore Jerusalem was immediately placed together, for again, the laws of the Medes and Persians cannot be changed (See Daniel 6:8,12,15; Esther 1:19).

This means, the command to build Jerusalem was always there once it was stated and issued by king Cyrus, and so, when king Artaxerxes made the decree to restore Jerusalem to the Laws of God, all was then fulfilled, (See Note B) for the Hebrew word translated in the text of the prophecy as "restore", means restore to control, not restore as in building (See 2 Kings 14:22; 1 Kings 20:34; 1 Kings 12:21; Judges 11:13; also see Isaiah 1:26), thus, we can see how when king Artaxerxes made the final half of the decree that restored the Laws of God to Jerusalem, how all was fulfilled in ,"from the going forth of the commandment to build and restore Jerusalem" in 457 B.C. by king Artaxerxes, as we also discuss in greater detail in the book "The Forgotten Faith of Jesus".

Now we learn from Holy Writ (See Luke 3:1,21-22; Acts 10:38), that the Messiah, my Lord and Savior Jesus Christ, was anointed as the Messiah at Baptism (for Messiah means "anointed one") in the fifteenth year of the reign of Tiberius Caeser, which history informs us was A.D. 27, Thus, when we take the secular date for king Artaxerxes of 457 B.C. which is the start point for the "going forth of the commandment to restore and to build Jerusalem unto the Messiah the Prince" and add the end point of A.D. 27 together, we get the exact total years of the Prophecy of Daniel 9:25, that is, 483 years. For 457 B.C. + A.D. 27 -1*= 483 years total (See Note A).

It should be pointed out that while Tiberius became sole ruler of the Roman Empire in A.D. 14, he had previously been made the co-ruler with Augustus over the provinces of the Roman Empire in A.D. 12. Thus the first year of Tiberius Caeser in "the country about Jordan" where John the Baptist, who Baptized our Lord Jesus Christ, was baptizing, would be A.D. 12, thus the fifteenth year of Tiberius Caeser would be A.D. 27.

Now when we look at the oldest portion of the Dead Sea Scrolls Book of Daniel (Around 125 B.C.) we see that this means, that the prophecy, using secular dates, places the event for the arrival and coming of the Messiah, my Lord and Savior Jesus Christ, as being written 151 years before the event occurred (125 B.C. + A.D. 27 -1 = 151 years total), which is impossible to have happened under human hands, but not under The Divine Hand, for as my God and Savior Jesus Christ Himself has stated: "And now, I have told you before it come to pass, that, when it is come to pass, ye might believe. (John 14:29 See Isaiah 46:9-10) Therefore, let us believe, for the impossibility of revealing history before it has happened is possible through the utterance of God as we have see, for through the power and direction of God, nothing is impossible, even revealing and recording down history over a century before it has happened, and this using dates that are even to skeptical for the skeptics themselves! This indeed proves the existence of God and the truth of Christianity. Therefore, let us believe in God, and follow Christ Jesus our Lord to salvation and life everlasting. Amen.

Note A: (*You have to subtract (-1) one when adding B.C. and A.D. dates together because there is no "Zero Year")

Note B: We see that king Artaxerxes commanded Ezra to fulfill the Laws of God (See Ezra 7:25-26), and since part of the Laws of God command for sacrifices to be made, (See Ezra 7:11-26; Isaiah 1:26; 1 Samuel 15:22), but sacrifices are only pleasing to God when the walls of Jerusalem have been built (See Psalm 51:18-19), therefore to fulfill the command of king Artaxerxes to fulfill the Law of God which requires sacrifices, the wall of Jerusalem must also be built, and so king Artaxerxes in this way, also issued a command to build Jerusalem by issuing the command to fulfill the Laws of God, which as we showed above is how "restore" was fulfilled, (See 1 Kings 20:34; Judges 11:13; 1 Kings 12:21; 2 Kings 14:22). That is, by king

Artaxerxes giving the command to administer the Laws of God, he fulfilled the "restore" portion of the prophecy of Daniel as we discussed above. (See Isaiah 1:26; Ezra 4:12-13; Ezra 7:15; Ezra 7:26; Ezra 6:14; Ezra 9:9; Zechariah 1:16).

55

WHAT REALLY HAPPENS WHEN WE DIE ACCORDING TO THE BIBLE?

What is what one of the greatest mysteries of life? The answer of course is Death. So then what happens when we die? What is death like according to The Bible? And The Biblically answer is: That when someone is dead, that person has no mental function until the resurrection of the dead at the Second Coming of Christ Jesus our Lord. (See Acts 24:15; Luke 14:14; 1 Thessalonians 4:16-17; Revelation 20:4-6) We read: "For what is your life? It is even a vapour, that appeareth for a little time, and then vanisheth away. (James 4:14) For the living know that they shall die: but the dead know not any thing, (Ecclesiastes 9:5) for "All things come alike to all: there is one event to the righteous, and to the wicked; to the good and to the clean, and to the unclean; to him that sacrificeth, and to him that sacrificeth not: as is the good, so is the sinner; and he that sweareth, as he that feareth an oath. This is an evil among all things that are done under the sun, that there is one event unto all: yea, also the heart of the sons of men is full of evil, and madness is in their heart while they live, and after that they go to the dead. (Ecclesiastes 9:2-3).

Therefore, seeing that all die, and that in death we have no mental function according to Scripture (See Ecclesiastes 9:5; Psalms 146:4), we come very naturally to one question that will plague the minds of all who have been taught that a person upon death goes to either heaven or hell, that is, Do we not naturally have an immortal soul within us that cannot die? And Holy Writ responds, that No, mankind has no immortal Soul, for only God is immortal (Compare 1 Timothy 6:14-16; 1 Timothy 1:17), while mankind on the other hand, is mortal (See Job 4:17), and is to seek for immortality (See Romans 2:7), which is only available through Christ Jesus our Lord alone

(See John 11:25-26; 1 John 5:11-13; Romans 6:23; also John 11:11-14; Job 19:25-27).

So then what is the Soul of man? The soul of man, the human sole that is, is man himself, for man has no soul within him, rather he is himself a soul (See Genesis 2:7; also Job 7:15; Genesis 19:19-20), and as we read specifically, the soul can be dead (See Revelation 16:3; Ezekiel 18:20; James 5:20), So then, what is the human "spirit", which is of course the next question, and rightly so. And Scripture responds that the human spirit (translated as "breath" in Psalms 146:4) is the human mind (See and Compare Romans 7:22-23; Ephesians 3:16-17,20; 1 Kings 21:7; 1 Kings 21:5; that reveals that the inward man is the mind, and the mind is the heart, and the heart is the spirit, also Compare Romans 7:22-23; Ephesians 3:16-17,20; Zechariah 12:1; also Compare Psalm 146:4; Genesis 6:5; Jeremiah 17:9-10; Ezekiel 38:10; Daniel 2:29; also Compare Psalm 146:4; Zechariah 12:1; Psalm 103:14; Ecclesiastes 12:7; Genesis 2:7; Ezekiel 38:10; Daniel 2:29).

Which (the spirit, which is the mind) when separated from someone, the person ceases to have mental cognition and thoughts, as we find revealed in Psalms 146:4 were the same Hebrew word for "spirit" is translated as "breath". Man it should be pointed out, is, as Scripture says, the dust portion of the equation of life, not the soul or spirit portion, just to make the point even clearer (See Ecclesiastes 3:18-20; also Genesis 2:7; Genesis 3:19; Psalm 103:14). And again, since God is a Spirit (See John 4:24), and only God has immortality (See 1 Timothy 6:14-16; 1 Timothy 1:17), this means that only God is an immortal Spirit.

So, in conclusion, what happens when we die according to The Bible? We go into the sleep of death (See John 11:11-14; 1 Corinthians 15:20), until the resurrection (See 1 Thessalonians 4:16-17), and so we remain until we are called out of death, however, while during death we have no thoughts and know nothing, which means we experience nothing, and have no feeling sensation, or gain any "hidden wisdom" as some people may believe.

Now, the next question we naturally come to is: What happens to the wicked, that is, those who do not turn to Christ Jesus our Lord for forgiveness of sin, and eternal life? It is commonly believed that the unrighteous and wicked will be forever in eternal torment in the fires of a never ending hell, yet this is not what Holy Scripture reveals within its pages. For consider, the wicked are consigned to the Second Death (See Revelation 21:8), which is very important, for as Scripture reveals, "the dead know not any thing, (Ecclesiastes 9:5 See Psalm 146:4), which means they will have no feeling upon the fires of hell fulfilling their work of administering the punishment for sin which is death (Consider Romans 6:16,23; James 5:20; 1 John 5:11-13).

And we know that the fires of hell will not be tormenting the wicked for all eternity, both because God specifically states through His Holy Word that the wicked will be burned up, (See Matthew 10:28; Matthew 3:12; Psalm 37:9-11,20), for only the righteous will abide forever (See 1 John 2:17).

And because the example of the eternal fires of hell, is that of the fire that destroyed Sodom and Gomorrha, which itself destroyed the wicked and turned them to ashes. We read: "Even as Sodom and Gomorrha, and the cities about them in like manner, giving themselves over to fornication, and going after strange flesh, are set forth as an example, suffering the vengeance of eternal fire. (Jude 7) But the same day that Lot went out of Sodom it rained fire and brimstone from heaven, and destroyed them all. (Luke 17:29) And turning the cities of Sodom and Gomorrha into ashes condemned them with an overthrow, making them an ensample unto those that after should live ungodly; (2 Peter 2:6 See Lamentations 4:6),

Which again, shows that the wicked that are consigned to the Second Death, face a death that is exactly like the First Death that all of humanity faces at this moment, and since in this First Death there is no mental thinking power for the dead, for they know nothing as Scripture states (See Ecclesiastes 9:5; Psalm 146:4), we can know that the wicked will totally be burned up and destroyed, and not writhing around in constant pain and torment for all eternity. "For evildoers shall be cut off: but those that wait upon the LORD, they shall inherit the earth. For yet a little while, and the wicked shall not be: yea, thou shalt diligently consider his place, and it shall not be. But the meek shall inherit the earth; and shall delight themselves in the abundance of peace. (Psalm 37:9-11) But the wicked shall perish, and the enemies of the LORD shall be as the fat of lambs: they shall consume; into smoke shall they consume away. (Psalm 37:20) For the wages of sin is death; but the gift of God is eternal life through Jesus Christ our Lord. (Romans 6:23).

Now, there are still going to be countless objections to the fact that Scripture states that the wicked will be utterly destroyed and not in constant torment for all eternity, which is why we recommend you get our book "What Happens When You Die", that deals with these important issues and objections which this brief introductory book cannot do without becoming a long dissertation on the subject like that book is. Amen.

THE LAW OF GOD AND THE SEVENTH-DAY SABBATH

Here is the patience of the saints: here are they that keep the commandments of God, and the faith of Jesus. (Revelation 14:12) With this one passage from Holy Writ alone that is describing those who are the saints of our God, we can come immediately to the realization that Christians, that is, all who are faithful to God and our Lord Jesus Christ, must indeed keep The Law of God, which are The Commandments of God. It will be objected however, that Christians are not obligated to keep The Law of God because Scripture declares in (Colossians 2:14 See Ephesians 2:15) that we are no longer under this command for it reads: "Blotting out the handwriting of ordinances that was against us, which was contrary to us, and took it out of the way, nailing it to his cross;".

Now this indeed seems to indicate that The Law of God is no longer in effect, however, when we Study The Bible as we are commanded to do (See 2 Timothy 2:15; 2 Timothy 3:16-17; Romans 15:4; Compare Ephesians 6:17; 1 Corinthians 2:13; John 6:63) we come to a different conclusion. For our Lord Jesus Christ hath indeed declared: "Think not that I am come to destroy the law, or the prophets: I am not come to destroy, but to fulfil. For verily I say unto you, Till heaven and earth pass, one jot or one tittle shall in no wise pass from the law, till all be fulfilled. (Matthew 5:17-18)

Now seeing that the New Heavens and New Earth discussed by Isaiah (66:22-24) the Prophet has not occurred as of yet, we can discern that not all has been fulfilled in The Law and The Prophets, therefore The Law of God is still in effect. The question now becomes: Is there a dichotomy in Scripture by us being commanded in one place in Holy Writ to keep The

Law, and in another place stating that it has been abolished? The answer is not at all, "For God is not the author of confusion, (1 Corinthians 14:33). So then what is The Biblical answer? That there are two sets of Law in Holy Writ, The Law of God which is The Ten Commandments, and then the separate Law of Moses (See Deuteronomy 4:12-14; Deuteronomy 5:22; 2 Kings 21:8).

This means as we discover through Scripture, that The Law referred to in (Colossians 2:14; Ephesians 2:15) that has been done away with, is The Law of Moses, which again, is separate from The Law of Ten Commandments, for notice it says: "Blotting out the handwriting of ordinances that was against us". Only The Law of Moses was said to be against us in Scripture (See Deuteronomy 31:25-26; also Acts 15:5,10), which when we consider James (1:25; 2:10-12) that there is The Law of Liberty, this can only be The Law of Ten Commandments that is separate from The Law of Moses, for The Law of Moses being said to be against us and written by him and placed at the side of the Ark of The Covenant (See Deuteronomy 31:24-26), cannot be that which liberates us, which only leaves The Law of Ten Commandments which God wrote Himself (Compare Deuteronomy 4:12-14; Deuteronomy 5:22) and was placed inside The Ark of The Covenant (See 1 Kings 8:9) which is in Heaven (See Revelation 11:19; Consider Hebrews 8:5; Hebrews 9:23). For we read in James 2:10-12 the following: "For whosoever shall kept the whole law, and yet offend in one point, he is guilty of all. For he that said, Do not commit adultery, said also, Do not kill. Now if thou commit no adultery, yet if thou kill, thou art a transgressor of the law. So speak ye, and so do, as they that shall be judged by the law of liberty."

Which, as we can see, both of these commandments to not killing and not commit adultery are found in The Ten Commandments in Exodus 20:1-17, which again, when we consider that God places a separate distinction from His Laws and The Law of Moses (See 2 Kings 21:8), and Moses himself also places a distinction (Compare Deuteronomy 4:12-14; Deuteronomy 5:22), we can see that we are indeed commanded and required to keep all of The Ten Commandments: "For whosoever shall keep the whole law, and yet offend in one point, he is guilty of all. (James 2:10; See James 1:25; James 2:10-12; Romans 7:7,12; 1 Corinthians 7:19; Revelation 14:12; Ephesians 6:1-3; Romans 13:9; Compare Romans 3:31; Romans 6:16; 1 John 3:4).

Therefore, let us not be negligent or slothful in our duty towards God in obeying His Ten Commandments Law. For "Know ye not, that to whom ye yield yourselves servants to obey, his servants ye are to whom ye obey;

whether of sin unto death, or of obedience unto righteousness? (Romans 6:16) Whosoever committeth sin transgresseth also the law: for sin is the transgression of the law. (1 John 3:4) Here is the patience of the saints: here are they that keep the commandments of God, and the faith of Jesus. (Revelation 14:12) Therefore let us do so, let us keep The Ten Commandments Law of God so that we may indeed be those whom God declares to be His Saints.

Now even though we are required to keep The Ten Commandments as we have read, there is still going to be an objection to one of The Ten Commandments in particular, that is, The Fourth Commandment concerning The Seventh-day Sabbath. And so, let us ask the question: Are we as Bible believing Christians required to keep The Seventh-day Sabbath of God as contained in The Fourth Commandment? The answer is a resounding YES, as we can see from Holy Writ when we consider the following. We read: "There remaineth therefore a rest* to the people of God." (Hebrews 4:9) *"rest" Greek "Sabbatismos" which means "Sabbath Keeping" which we read in the margin of the King James Bible by the translators: "keeping of a sabbath", And what Sabbath must we keep? The answer is, we are to keep the same Sabbath as our Lord and Savior Jesus Christ. We read: "He that saith he abideth in him ought himself also so to walk, even as he walked. (1 John 2:6) For even hereunto were ye called: because Christ also suffered for us, leaving us an example, that ye should follow his steps: (1 Peter 2:21) And he came to Nazareth, where he had been brought up: and, as his custom was, he went into the synagogue on the sabbath day, and stood up for to read. (Luke 4:16). Now notice that it was the custom of our Lord and Savior Jesus Christ to keep The Sabbath, therefore we who follow His footsteps must also make it our custom. Furthermore our Lord Jesus Christ is Lord of The Sabbath (See Matthew 12:8; Mark 2:28; Luke 6:5), therefore The Lord's Day in Revelation 1:10 is The Seventh-day Sabbath. We also discover from Holy Writ that our Lord and Savior Jesus Christ is JEHOVAH (Compare (Compare Isaiah 40:3; Matthew 3:1-3; John 1:19-23; John 3:27-28), and The Seventh-day Sabbath is The Day of JEHOVAH (See Isaiah 58:13), for it is The Day in which He rested (See Exodus 20:8-11). Amen.

Now the question is: Are you going to walk as our Lord and Savior Jesus Christ walked by keeping the same Seventh-day Sabbath as He kept, or, are you going to follow the Sabbath of your own creation? The choice is yours "but as for me an my house, we will serve the LORD. (Joshua 24:15). Which brings us to our next point, Holy Writ reveals that we are to obey our Lord and Savior Jesus Christ if we are to obtain salvation (See Hebrews 5:9; Compare Romans 6:16; 1 John 3:4), which of course brings us to the discussion of how faith and works combine in Scripture, which is indeed a very important question that every Christian must seek an answer to, for if we do not fully discover this answer from Holy Writ, we may be lead into thinking that we need only believe in Christ without actually obeying Him and following Him, which should not be, especially when we have the plainest declaration against that folly through Holy Writ as we read: "Thou believest that there is one God; thou doest well: the devils also believe, and tremble. But wilt thou know, O vain man, that faith without works is dead? (James 2:19-20 See James 2:15-23) For our Lord Jesus Christ "became the author of eternal salvation unto all them that obey him; (Hebrews 5:9 See Matthew 7:21; Matthew 12:30; Romans 6:16; John 14:24).

Now the question becomes, seeing that we read: "Then said they unto him, What shall we do, that we might work the works of God? Jesus answered and said unto them, This is the work of God, that ye believe on him whom he hath sent. (John 6:28-29) What exactly is the relationship between faith and obedience to works that we are commanded to do in Scripture, seeing that the work we must do is have belief in Christ Jesus our Lord, as have we just read here in John 6:28-29?

And the answer is: That while works do not bestow upon us merit for it is actually God doing the good works through you, you are however damned if you do not follow through with obedience to God, thus works, for if you do not do the works, this is considered that you are in rebellion to what God hath said to do, which is considered that you are an unbeliever, that is, if you are in rebellion to what God says to do and commands then you are considered an unbeliever, which means, since only those who believe are saved (See John 3:16-18), that if you do not do the works that you are commanded to do in Scripture then you are an unbeliever, which is why we read in Scripture that you are both justified by faith alone (See Romans 4:2; Romans 4:1-5; also Romans 4:20-25; Ephesians 2:8-10), (for the works cannot save you because they are an obligation See Luke 17:10, for it is actually God doing the good works through you See Philippians 2:13), and that you are justified because of works (See James 2:21; James 2:24; Also James 2:20-26; Hebrews 11:8; Titus 3:8), because, if you do not do the works, this is equated with you being in rebellion to what God hath said, which is equated with being an unbeliever (Compare Numbers 20:12; Numbers 20:24; Context Numbers 20:7-13; Numbers 20:23-24; Also See 1 Samuel 15:23), of course mere doing of the works without faith and belief in Christ Jesus our Lord is worthless, because salvation is only obtained through belief in Him alone (See John 3:16-18).

Now let us unpack these points. First: Good works do not bestow upon us merit for it is actually God doing the works through you. We read: "So likewise ye, when ye shall have done all those things which are commanded you, say, We are unprofitable servants: we have done that which was our duty to do. (Luke 17:10) For it is God which worketh in you both to will and to do of his good pleasure. (Philippians 2:13 See 1 Corinthians 15:10)

Second: We must do the good works of obedience that God hath commanded in Holy Writ or we are in rebellion to His Word which is considered that one is an unbeliever. We read: "And Samuel said, Hath the LORD as great delight in burnt offerings and sacrifices, as in obeying the voice of the LORD? Behold, to obey is better than sacrifice, and to hearken then the fat of rams. For rebellion is as the sin of witchcraft, and stubbornness is as iniquity and idolatry. Because thou hast rejected the word of the LORD, he hath also rejected thee from being king. (1 Samuel 15:22-23) And the LORD spake unto Aaron and Moses, **Because ye believed me not,** to sanctify me in the eyes of the children of Israel, therefore ye shall not bring this congregation into the land which I have given them. (Numbers 20:12) Aaron shall be gathered unto his people: for he shall not enter into the land which I have given unto the children of Israel, **because ye rebelled against my word** at the waters of Meribah. (Numbers 20:24; See Context Numbers 20:7-13; Numbers 20:23-24)

Third: One must believe in Christ Jesus our Lord or you will not receive salvation. We read: "For God so loved the world, that he gave his only begotten Son, that whosoever believeth in him should not perish, but have everlasting life. For God sent not his Son into the world to condemn the world; but that the world through him might be saved. He that believeth on him is not condemned: but he that believeth not is condemned already, because he hath not believed in the name of the only begotten Son of God. (John 3:16-18).

Fourth: We perfectly see the relationship between faith and works by the example of Abraham in the following. We read: "By faith Abraham, when he was called to go out into a place which he should after receive for an inheritance, obeyed; and he went out, not knowing whither he went. (Hebrews 11:8). Therefore dear and beloved reader, let us not forsake our duty to Christ Jesus our Lord to both believe in Him, and Walk with Him unto Heavenly Jerusalem, for we must have faith in Him, and this faith must be more then simple mental assent that He is our Lord and Savior, but actual physical obedience, for as He Himself has stated: "He that is not with me is against me; and he that gathereth not with me scattereth abroad. (Matthew 12:30).

Now as we come to our final point in this chapter, it well might be declared by some, that they are be judged by me, by us pointing out what Scripture itself is revealing, and they themselves might state that Scripture itself declares that judgment should not take place concerning themselves (See Matthew 7:1-2), yet is this indeed what Holy Writ is revealing? Let us discover together. And so we read: "Judge not, that ye be not judged. For with what judgment ye judge, ye shall be judged: and with what measure ye meter, it shall be measured to you again." in (Matthew 7:1-2) And so, the question does indeed become, What does this truly mean and entail? For consider, if we are to both do that which we have read in this passage, and we are also to call others away from sin as James (5:20) states, that says: "Let him know, that he which converteth the sinner from the error of his way shall save a soul from death, and shall hide a multitude of sins." how can we truly and Biblically do both? How can we point out sin without judging? The answer should be obvious, "Judge not, that ye be not judged." is referring to our own private opinions on things, that is, if we place a unbiblical standard on something, such as we say, "Watching TV is a sin", if we turn around and then watch TV, we ourselves will be judged as transgressors and sinners by that same standard that we set up, for as Holy Writ declares, if you think something is a sin, then it is a sin for you, as we can see from the very passage of (Matthew 7:1-2) in comparison with (Romans 14:23).

However, there is a standard of judgment that all are subject to whether they like it or not, and that standard is what The Bible declares. For we read: "All scripture is given by inspiration of God, and is profitable for doctrine, for reproof, for correction, for instruction in righteousness: That the man of God may be perfect, thoroughly furnished unto all good works. (2 Timothy 3:16-17). Now notice this, we specifically read: "All scripture is given …. for reproof" that is, The Bible is the standard of judgment, which means that it does not matter if one judges by this standard or not, for in the end, you will be judged by this standard no matter what you say or do, which means we indeed can call others and ourselves away from sins and towards righteousness as James states, for we can indeed point out that something is a sin, for indeed we are not judging someone, we are simply quoting what God says on the subject, that is all. Amen.

The Ten Commandments Of God

And God spake all these words, saying, I am the LORD thy God, which have brought thee out of the land of Egypt, out of the house of bondage. Thou shalt have no other gods before me. Thou shalt not make unto thee any graven image, or any likeness of any thing that is in heaven above, or that is in the earth beneath, or that is in the water under the earth. Thou shalt not bow down thyself to them, nor serve them: for I the LORD thy God am a jealous God, visiting the iniquity of the fathers upon the children unto the third and fourth generation of them that hate me; And shewing mercy unto thousands of them that love me, and keep my commandments. Thou shalt not take the name of the LORD thy God in vain; for the LORD will not hold him guiltless that taketh his name in vain. Remember the sabbath day, to keep it holy. Six days shalt thou labour, and do all thy work: But the seventh day is the sabbath of the LORD thy God: in it thou shalt not do any work, thou, nor thy son, nor the daughter, thy manservant, nor thy maidservant, nor thy cattle, nor thy stranger that is within thy gates: For in six days the LORD made heaven and earth, the sea, and all that in them is, and rested the seventh day: wherefore the LORD blessed the sabbath day, and hallowed it. Honour thy father and thy mother: that thy days may be long upon the land which the LORD thy God giveth thee. Thou shalt not kill. Thou shalt not commit adultery. Thou shalt not steal. Thou shalt not bear false witness against thy neighbour. Thou shalt not covet thy neighbour's house, thou shalt not covet thy neighbour's wife, nor his manservant, nor his maidservant, nor is ox, nor his ass, nor any thing that is thy neighbour's. (Exodus 20:1-17).

EVIDENCE FOR CHRISTIANITY

The proof of Christianity can be summed up in the simplest of ways. That is, that Holy Writ contains that which no mortal man could produce, which is the history of the rise and fall of empire being written down before it happened and happening exactly as it was declared in the Scriptures. We read in the book of the prophet Daniel, the second chapter, the history of the world declared before it occurred stating, that starting with Babylon that there would be three other kingdoms after it, that would supersede it, that is, four complete kingdoms in total starting with Babylon, and that the fourth kingdom would break apart into ten kingdoms, that is, the part of the territory of the fourth kingdom that was never part of the territory of the other three kingdoms that it conquered and occupied, would break apart into ten kingdoms. And history shows that all four kingdoms happened exactly as The Bible declared that they would, and that the ten kingdoms also occurred as Holy Writ stated, the important part being that the date that even the skeptics admit that The Book of Daniel was written, places this event of the ten kingdoms as being written 600 years before it happened and happening exactly as it was written, this proves that Christianity is true.

We read specifically from the prophecy of Daniel chapter two, that King Nebuchadnezzar (who's posterity is said to be part of his kingdom See Jeremiah 27:4-7; Jeremiah 25:11-14) was given a dream of world empire starting with his kingdom and ending with the eventual setting-up of the kingdom of God. This dream that was both retold to King Nebuchadnezzar and interpreted by the prophet Daniel by direction of God was and is the following: Nebuchadnezzar the King was shown an image in his dream, "This image's head was of fine gold, his breasts and his arms of silver, his belly and his thighs of brass, His legs of iron, and his feet part of iron and part of clay. (Daniel 2:32-33) The interpretation is as Scripture reveals that each of the metals represents a different Kingdom that supersedes the other Kingdom that came before it. For speaking to King Nebuchadnezzar the prophet Daniel reveals by inspiration of God that "Thou art this head of gold. And after thee shall arise another kingdom inferior to thee, and another third kingdom of brass, which shall bear rule over all the earth. And the fourth kingdom shall be strong as iron: (Daniel 2:38-40)

The posterity of King Nebuchadnezzar are all part of his kingdom (See Jeremiah 27:4-7; Jeremiah 25:11-14) which is important for we read declared to King Belshazzar who is of the posterity of King Nebuchadnezzar "Thy kingdom is divided, and given to the Medes and Persians. (Daniel 5:28) Thus the silver represents the combined Medes and Persians, just as the gold represents Babylon. We see specifically that the Medes and Persians are considered as one kingdom in the prophecy of Daniel 8:3-4,20. Secular history points out that Babylon was conquered by the Medes and Persians as is revealed through ancient historians and through the Cyrus Cylinder.

The third kingdom of brass is the Greeks, for as we can read in the Prophecy of Daniel Eight, the Medes and Persians (Daniel 8:3-4,20) are supersede and conquered by the Greeks (Daniel 8:5-8,21-22), Secular history reveals that the decisive battle over the Medes and Persians was made by the Greeks through Alexander the Great at the battle of Arbela. The fourth kingdom of Iron is the Romans (See Luke 2:1) who as secular history shows made their decisive victory over the Greeks at the battle of Pydna.

We read now that which is stated about the Iron kingdom of Rome, for it is said not that it would be conquered, but that it would simply brake apart, as is declared: "And the fourth kingdom shall be as strong as iron: forasmuch as iron breaketh in pieces and subdueth all things: and as iron that breaketh all these, shall it break in pieces and bruise. And whereas thou sawest the feet and toes, part of potters' clay, and part of iron, the kingdom shall be divided; but there shall be in it of the strength of the iron, forasmuch as thou sawest the iron mixed with miry clay. And as the toes of the feet were part of iron, and part of clay, so the kingdom shall be partly strong, and partly broken. And whereas thou sawest iron mixed with miry clay, they shall mingle themselves with the seed of men: but they shall not cleave one to another, even as iron is not mixed with clay. (Daniel 2:40-43) The Iron kingdom of Rome broke apart into two main kingdoms as history attests. The kingdom of the Eastern Roman empire at Constantinople, and the kingdom of the Western Roman empire at Rome in Italy.

The Western Roman empire broke apart into ten kingdoms through the barbarian invasion of the western Roman empire, just as the prophecy of Daniel two states that it would. The ten kingdoms or ten toes are as follows, as secular history reveals unto us:

1. Anglo-Saxons (England)
2. Franks (France)
3. Burgundians (Switzerland)
4. Visigoths (Spain)
5. Alamanni (Germany)
6. Suevi (Portugal)
7. Lombards (Italy)
8. Heruli (Destroyed A.D. 493)
9. Vandals (Destroyed A.D. 534)
10. Ostrogoths (Destroyed A.D. 538)

Now the reason it is said that the ten toes, that is, ten kingdoms come from the Western Roman empire are twofold. First: The parallel Prophecy of Daniel Seven that gives more detail reveals such (See Daniel 7:3-7,11-12,23). Second: Since the Iron and Clay toes are exactly that, Iron and Clay, that is, they are not Iron, Clay, Gold, Silver, and Brass, this means that the ten toes, that is, ten kingdoms are all part of the territory of the Roman Empire that was never part of the territory of the Gold (Babylon), Silver (Medes and Persians), Brass (Greeks), for the statue of Daniel two remains intact until its destruction at the end of the world, that is, the metals remain separate and not mixed together.

In the Prophecy of Daniel Seven we find that there are four beasts. The First: is a lion with eagles wings. Second: is a bear. Third: a leopard with four heads with four wings of a fowl. Fourth: a strange beast that has ten horns. (See Daniel 7:3-9) We find in prophecy that a beast represents a kingdom (See Daniel 7:23) and horns represent kingdoms (See Daniel 8:8,21-22).

This prophecy of Daniel 7 was made during the Kingdom of Babylon during the reign of King Belshazzar, which is important, for since the posterity of King Nebuchadnezzar are part of his kingdom (See Jeremiah 27:4-7; Jeremiah 25:11-14) and Belshazzar is one of his descendants (See Daniel 5:1,10-11) this means both kings represent the kingdom of Babylon, which in-itself is significant, for the only two places we read "fourth kingdom" in all of Scripture is concerning the Iron in Daniel 2 that we established was the Roman kingdom, and here in Daniel 7:23 concerning the fourth beast. Thus working our way back starting with the fourth beast, we see that the fourth beast is the Romans, the third beast is the Greeks, the second beast is the Medes and Persians, and the first beast is the Babylonians. There are also other parallels that show this is so in Scripture that we discuss in the book "The Forgotten Faith of Jesus".

Now here is the point, the fourth beast has ten horns coming from its head, and horns as The Bible points out represent kingdoms (See Daniel 8:8,21-22), and since the other three beasts are separate from the fourth beast (See Daniel 7:12) and these other three beasts represent and controlled territories that were part of the Eastern Roman empire, this leaves only the Western Roman empire for the ten horns, that is, kingdoms to come from, which we have discussed who they are above.

Now according to secular science*, the oldest portion of the Dead Sea Scrolls of the Book of Daniel is dated to around 125 B.C. and the ten kingdoms that occurred in the Western Roman empire happened in A.D. 476. Thus using secular dates, we find that according to history and science, that the prophecy in the book of Daniel was written 600 years before it happened, and happened exactly as it was written. This is the evidence for Christianity, for as my Lord and Savior Jesus Christ hath declared: "And now, I have told you before it come to pass, that, when it is come to pass, ye might believe. (John 14:29 See Isaiah 46:9-10) Therefore let us believe, and let us be saved through Christ from the sins and despair of this life that so engulfs us like a drowning man in the depths of the sea, for as we have seen, the impossibility of revealing world history before it hath occurred is possible by the everlasting Hand of God. Amen.

*See "The Meaning Of The Dead Sea Scrolls By James VanderKam & Peter Flint 2002 t & t clark" Pages 137-138

THE SECOND COMING OF CHRIST ACCORDING TO SCRIPTURE

The Christians great hope is our being forgiven of our sins and being reconciled to God though Christ Jesus our Lord which we have discussed previously. Our other great hope is that our Lord and Savior Jesus Christ will come again to raise us and take us unto Himself into the clouds (See 1 Thessalonians 4:16-17), and then into the paradise of God into heaven itself for one thousand years (See Revelation 20:4-6), which after this is accomplished, God will bring us back to this earth were He will judge the wicked and administer the punishment for sin which is death eternal upon them (See Revelation 20:1-15; Revelation 21:8; Romans 6:23; 1 John 5:11-13; John 3:16-18; 1 John 2:17), and then God will dwell with us on this earth that He recreates (See Revelation 21:1-4; Isaiah 65:17; Isaiah 66:22-23; 2 Peter 3:10-13).

Now Scripture makes it very clear that while we can never know exactly when our Lord and Savior Jesus Christ will return (See Matthew 24:35-36; Matthew 25:1-13; Mark 13:31-32), we can discern that it is near even at the door (See Matthew 24:32-33; Mark 13:28-29). Now, while we are not going to discuss the seven last plagues of Revelation (15:1-8; 16:1-21), which at the time of this writing have not as yet been fulfilled, what we are going to discuss however, is some of the Signs of the End Times that have been fulfilled, and then the declarations of our Lord Jesus Christ that He will return to this earth and raise the righteous dead to Him in the clouds of heaven, and that the righteous living will be caught up also, while the wicked will be slain at His coming and shall await in the sleep of death until after the thousand year millennium, which after this time, the judgment of the wicked shall take place, and their punishment of eternal death administered by fire, of which they shall never be anymore, for they will be forever in the sleep and oblivion of death will take place. We shall also discuss how the Secret Rapture doctrine is unbiblical.

The Signs Of The End Times That Have Been Fulfilled

This know also, that in the last days perilous times shall come. For men shall be lovers of their own selves, covetous, boasters, proud, blasphemers, disobedient to parents, unthankful, unholy, Without natural affection, trucebreakers, false accusers, incontinent, fierce, despisers of those that are good, Traitors, heady, highminded, lovers of pleasure more than lovers of God; Having a form of godliness, but denying the power thereof: from such turn away. For of this sort are they which creep into houses, and lead captive silly woman laden with sins, led away with diverse lusts, Ever learning, and never able to come to the knowledge of the truth. (2 Timothy 3:1-7) This exhortation and warning to consider the signs of the end times must truly be the introduction to our Biblical discussion concerning the Second Coming of our Lord and Savior Jesus Christ, for as we are going to see from Holy Writ, many of the signs that show that we are in the Time of The End are fulfilled, especially that we are living in the days of Noah and Lot when our Lord and Savior Jesus Christ said the He shall return.

But before we consider this from Holy Scripture, consider first that the introduction to the end of days has been fulfilled. We read: "Tell us, when shall these things be? and what shall be the sign of thy coming, and of the end of the world? And Jesus answered and said unto them, Take heed that no man deceive you. For many shall come in my name, saying, I am Christ; and shall deceive many. And ye shall hear of wars and rumors of wars: see that ye be not troubled: for all these things must come to pass, but the end is not yet. For nation shall rise against nation, and kingdom against kingdom: and there shall be famines, and pestilences, and earthquakes, in diverse places. All these are the beginning of sorrows. (Matthew 24:3-8). All of these points have been fulfilled in our world, as anyone living at the time of this writing can easily discern. Note: In the portion of the prophecy that reads: "For nation shall rise against nation", the word translated as "nation" as we find in our Bibles, is from the Greek word "Ethnos" that can mean "people" or "race", as we find in the Wiclif translation that reads: "folk schulen rise togidre ayens folk"* that is, "folk should rise together against folk", folk meaning people. And as anyone can consider in these days of ours, people have been rising against each other by the abundance of rioting that hath taken place. That is, not just people from other countries being against each other, but people within the same country being against each other.

Now, let us consider that our Lord Jesus Christ hath declared that when we are living in the days of Noah and in the days of Lot that this is when He shall return (See Luke 17:26-30). In the days of Noah there was much physical violence with people thinking about violence (See Genesis 6:5,11-13), just as we see today, both by much rioting that has taken place and by the constant portrayal of violence on television and video games, which of course is what causes people to think about violence. In the days of Lot there was much filthy communication and behavior (See 2 Peter 2:7-8), and homosexuality (Compare Genesis 19:5; Ezekiel 16:49-50; Leviticus 18:22; also Deuteronomy 22:5; Revelation 21:8), which was done openly (See Isaiah 3:9), among the vast majority (See Genesis 19:4) of both young and old (See Genesis 19:4), of which they declared that they should not be judged for this behavior (See Genesis 19:9), just as we see in these our days.

We learn in Daniel chapter two that the finial ten kingdoms of the iron and clay toes (See Daniel 2:40-44) which is when God is going to return to set up His Kingdom that shall never end, has been fulfilled as we have shown in the chapter "Evidence For Christianity". We see declared in Holy Writ that God will punish those who are destroying the earth (See Revelation 11:18), and because of the massive amounts of pollution that we see because of simple greed and love for money, do we not here see that our world is being destroyed? Thus this has been fulfilled also. Therefore now, let us truly be watchful and mindful of the days we are living in, for the day of the coming of The Lord Jesus Christ will soon no doubt be upon us, and it should not overtake us as a thief in the night as Scripture says (See 1 Thessalonians 5:2-6; Matthew 24:32-33) for we must ever be watchful and diligent of His return, for indeed we are in the end times. Amen.

*Quoted From: "The English Hexapla: Exhibiting the Six Important English Translations of the New Testament Scriptures ; the Original Greek Text after Scholz Publisher London : Samuel Bagster and Sons 1841"

The Second Coming Of Christ Jesus Our Lord

For the Lord himself shall descend from heaven with a shout, with the voice of the archangel, and with the trump of God: and the dead in Christ shall rise first. Then we which are alive and remain shall be caught up together with them in the clouds, to meet the Lord in the air: and so shall we ever be with the Lord. (1 Thessalonians 4:16-17) This introductory quote concerning The Second Coming of our Lord and Savior Jesus Christ brings us to our discussion on the great Christian hope that God shall come again and raise us unto Himself into the paradise of God. We read where our Lord Jesus Christ declares: "Let not your heart be troubled: ye believe in God, believe also in me. In my Father's house are many mansions: If it were not so, I would have told you. I go to prepare a place for you. And if I go and prepare a place for you, I will come again, and receive you unto myself; that where I am, there ye may be also. (John 14:1-3) And when he had spoken these things, while they beheld, he was taken up; and a cloud received him out of their sight. And while they looked stedfastly toward heaven as he went up, behold, two men stood by them in white apparel; Which also said, Ye men of Galilee, why stand ye gazing up into heaven? this same Jesus, which is taken up from you into heaven, shall so come in like manner as ye have seen him go into heaven. (Acts 1:9-11)

Be patient therefore, brethren, unto the coming of the Lord. Behold, the husbandman waiteth for the precious fruit of the earth, and hath long patience for it, until he receive the early and latter rain. Be ye also patient; stablish your hearts: for the coming of the Lord draweth nigh. (James 5:7-8) For our conversation is in heaven; from whence also we look for the Saviour, the Lord Jesus Christ: Who shall change our vile body, that it may be fashioned like unto his glorious body, according to the working whereby he is able even to subdue all things unto himself. (Philippians 3:20-21) Repent ye therefore, and be converted, that your sins may be blotted out, when the times of refreshing shall come from the presence of the Lord. And he shall send Jesus Christ, which before was preached unto you: Whom the heavens must receive until the times of restitution of all things, which God hath spoken by the mouth of all his holy prophets since the world began. (Acts 3:19-21) Behold, he cometh with the clouds; and every eye shall see him, and they also which pierced him: and all kindreds of the earth shall wail because of him. Even so, Amen. (Revelation 1:7)

Now consider why our Lord Jesus Christ seems to be delaying His return. We read: "The Lord is not slack concerning his promise, as some men count slackness; but is longsuffering to us-ward, not willing that any should perish, but that all should come to repentance. (2 Peter 3:9) Marvel not at this: for the hour is coming, in the which all that are in the graves shall hear his voice, And shall come forth; they that have done good, unto the resurrection of life; and they that have done evil, unto the resurrection of damnation. (John 5:28-29), therefore "have hope towards God, that they themselves also allow, that there shall be a resurrection of the dead, both of the just and unjust. (Acts 24:15)

And when shall the wicked be resurrected, for as we have read, the righteous are resurrected into the clouds at The Second Coming of our Lord Jesus Christ (See 1 Thessalonians 4:16-17), and we find declared from Holy Writ, that when He returns the wicked living are destroyed and remain this way until The Judgment that is one thousand years later. We read: "But the day of the Lord will come as a thief in the night; in the which the heavens shall pass away with a great noise, and the elements shall melt with fervent heat, the earth also and the works that are therein shall be burned up. (2 Peter 3:10) For the Lord himself shall descend from heaven with a shout, with the voice of the archangel, and with the trump of God: and the dead in Christ shall rise first. Then we which are alive and remain shall be caught up together with them in the clouds, to meet the Lord in the air: and so shall we ever be with the Lord. (1 Thessalonians 4:16-17) And I saw thrones, and they sat upon them, and judgment was given unto them: and I saw the souls of them that were beheaded for the witness of Jesus, and for the word of God, and which had not worshiped the beast, neither his image, neither had received his mark upon their foreheads, or in their hands; and they lived and reigned with Christ a thousand years. But the rest of the dead lived not again until the thousand years were finished. This is the first resurrection. Blessed and holy is he that hath part in the first resurrection: on such the second death hath no power, but they shall be priests of God and of Christ, and shall reign with him a thousand years. (Revelation 20:4-6)

For we must all appear before the judgment seat of Christ; that every one may receive the things done in his body, according to that he hath done, whether it be good or bad. (2 Corinthians 5:10) For the Son of man shall come in the glory of his Father with his angels; and then he shall reward every man according to his works. (Matthew 16:27) But I say unto you, That every idle word that men shall speak, they shall give account thereof in the day of judgment. For by thy words thou shalt be justified, and by thy words thou shalt be condemned. (Matthew 12:36-37) For the wages of sin is death; but the gift of God is eternal life through Jesus Christ our Lord. (Romans 6:23)

More Texts: (Luke 14:14; Acts 24:15; Matthew 22:30-31; Luke 20:35-36; John 5:28-29; John 11:25; 1 Corinthians 2:9)

The Final Punishment Of Eternal Death Upon The Wicked

For the wages of sin is death; but the gift of God is eternal life through Jesus Christ our Lord. (Romans 6:23) He that hath the Son hath life; and he that hath not the Son of God hath not life. (1 John 5:12) These two quotes from Holy Writ should indeed show that there are going to be only two types of people after The Judgment of all flesh rendered by Christ Jesus our Lord upon this world. That is, The Living and The Dead. Therefore, let us consider the punishment of the wicked, that is those sentenced to death. We read: "But the fearful, and unbelieving, and the abominable, and murderers, and whoremongers, and sorcerers, and idolaters, and all liars, shall have their part in the lake which burneth with the fire and brimstone: which is the second death. (Revelation 21:8)

Now let us consider this "second death" specifically, for it should indeed be exactly like the first death we all face, otherwise it would not be the second death. Therefore let us consider what takes place upon death. We read: "For the living know that they shall die: but the dead know not any thing, neither have they any more a reward; for the memory of them is forgotten. (Ecclesiastes 9:5) His breath goeth forth, he returneth to his earth; in that very day his thoughts perish. (Psalm 146:4)

Therefore we know from Holy Scripture that the wicked will not be in constant and eternal torment as some believe, rather they will be in forever death, and seeing as in death we "know not any thing" as we have read, for the "thoughts perish", this means that the wicked cannot be in torment, for then they would know it, which is the opposite of what death is were you know nothing, that is, if they were in pain they would know that it hurts and that that it is continuing to hurt, which means they are able to think this and know this, which again, would mean that they were not dead but alive, which goes against what Scripture declares that they shall be dead.

Furthermore, only those who do the will of God are said to abide forever (See 1 John 2:17; also Romans 6:16), which means if the wicked are in eternal torment then they are also abiding forever, which also goes against what Holy Writ declares shall be their fate, for the wicked indeed shall face the punishment for sins which is death as Scripture reveals and we have read, and they will be turned into ashes, and consumed away nevermore to ever be ever again. "For evildoers shall be cut off: but those that wait upon the LORD, they shall inherit the earth. For yet a little while, and the wicked shall not be: yea, thou shalt diligently consider his place, and it shall not be. But the meek shall inherit the earth; and shall delight themselves in the abundance of peace. (Psalm 37:9-11) But the wicked shall perish, and the enemies of the LORD shall be as the fat of lambs: they shall consume; into smoke shall they consume away. (Psalm 37:20; Compare Jude 7; Luke 17:29; 2 Peter 2:6). Amen.

Note: The wicked face the "second death" (See Revelation 21:8; Revelation

20:6; Revelation 20:14; Revelation 2:11), and the Greek word for "death" here in "second death" is Thanatos which is important, for we find this word directly linked to the Hebrew word Muth by The New Testament quoting from The Old Testament (Compare Mark 7:10; Exodus 21:17), that is, the Greek Thanatos is the Hebrew Muth and this is important, for in Ecclesiastes 9:5 "die" and "dead" are translated from the Hebrew Muth and in Ecclesiastes 9:5 this shows that the dead have no thoughts or thinking power for they "know not any thing", meaning, the wicked who are consigned to the "second death" that is, the second Thanatos which is the second Muth are not in a state of conscious torment, rather, they are in thoughtless death, for consider, if you are in torment and in pain you would know it, meaning, "it hurts", "it still hurts", "it is continuing to hurt" which is the opposite of what is declared to be death were you know nothing as we have read.

More Texts: (2 Peter 2:9; Matthew 12:36; Romans 14:10-12; Romans 6:23; Revelation 21:8; 1 John 2:17; Matthew 25:31-46; Psalm 37:9-11,20)

The Unbiblical Nature Of The Secret Rapture

Biblically, there is no such thing as the "secret rapture", or "rapture" mentioned in The Bible, what is mentioned however, which is apparently used to try to convince people of this notion that our Lord will one day secretly rapture away people, that is, they will simply disappear, then three and a half, or seven years later He will come openly, is the abuse of the text of Scripture that our Lord Jesus Christ will come as a "thief in the night", yet when we consider these two passages from Holy Writ in context, we learn from the one that it is referring that people are not being watchful of His return for Christians should not have His coming overtake them as a thief, and then from the second passage when He comes as the thief in the night, the entire world and universe will be burned up, as we read: "But of the times and the seasons, brethren ye have no need that I write unto you. For yourselves know perfectly that the day of the Lord so cometh as a thief in the nigh. For when they shall say, Peace and safety; then sudden destruction cometh upon them, as travail upon a woman with child; and they shall not escape. But ye, brethren, are not in darkness, that that day should overtake you as a thief. (1 Thessalonians 5:1-4) But the day of the Lord will come as a thief in the night; in the which the heavens shall pass away with a great noise, and the elements shall melt with fervent heat, the earth also and the works that are therein shall be burned up. (2 Peter 3:10)

Now consider specifically, that when our Lord Jesus Christ returns that all will see Him thus there is no "secret rapture". We read: "Behold, he cometh with the clouds; and every eye shall see him, and they also which pierced him: and all kindreds of the earth shall wail because of him. Even so, Amen. (Revelation 1:7). It should also be pointed out that when our Lord Jesus Christ returns that He will not set foot upon this earth, thus anyone claming to be Him is defiantly a fake, for when He returns the righteous will be caught up to Him in the clouds of heaven, of which there will be a great shout and trumpet of His return. We read: "For the Lord himself shall descend from heaven with a shout, with the voice of the archangel, and with the trump of God: and the dead in Christ shall rise first. Then we which are alive and remain shall be caught up together with them in the clouds, to meet the Lord in the air: and so shall we ever be with the Lord. (1 Thessalonians 4:16-17). Therefore, in conclusion of these text, we can conclude that the secret rapture doctrine is indeed unbiblical. Amen.

CONCLUSION

Therefore leaving the principles of the doctrine of Christ, let us go on unto perfection; not laying again the foundation of repentance from dead works, and faith towards God, Of the doctrine of baptism, and of laying on of hands, and of resurrection of the dead, and of eternal judgment. And this will we do, if God permit. (Hebrews 6:1-3) For "All scripture is given by inspiration of God, and is profitable for doctrine, for reproof, for correction, for instruction in righteousness: That the man of God may be perfect, thoroughly furnished unto all good works. (2 Timothy 3:16-17) Therefore "Study to shew thyself approved unto God, a workman that needeth not to be ashamed, rightly dividing the word of truth. (2 Timothy 2:15) And so dear reader, let us do so, let us ever take The Holy Words of God unto ourselves and prayerfully read them and study them, for they are indeed our guide to perfection that leads to the heavenly and everlasting Kingdom of God our Savior.

God be bless forevermore,

Amen.

NECESSARY READING

Through wisdom is an house builded; and by understanding it is established.   And by knowledge shall the chambers be filled with all precious and pleasant riches. Proverbs 24:3-4 King James Version.

The Book :

1. The Holy Bible

Books :

2. Bible Readings For The Home Circle
   By Unknown 1914 Review and Herald Publishing Association

3. Seventh-day Adventists Answer Questions on Doctrine
   Prepared by a Representative Group of Seventh-day Adventist Leaders,
   Bible Teachers, and Editors 1957 Review and Herald Publishing
   Association

4. Seventh-day Adventists Believe ... : A Biblical Exposition of 27
   Fundamental Doctrines By Ministerial Association General Conference
   of Seventh-day Adventists 1988 Review and Herald Publishing
   Association

5. Daniel : A closer look at the book that tells what will happen in the end
   times. By Kenneth Cox 2009 Remnant Publications

6. The Antichrist
   By Lawrence M. Nelson 1996 CHJ Publishing

7. Facsimiles Of The Two Earliest S.D.A. Periodicals
By Review And Herald Publishing Association

8. Bible Answers
By Review And Herald Publishing Association

9. Strong's Exhaustive Concordance Of The Bible With Greek And
Hebrew Dictionary By James Strong 1990 Regal Publishing Inc.

10. The Faithful Witness
By Sharon Thomas Crews 2003 Amazing Facts, Inc.

11. Bible Manual For Soul-Winners: Helps For Preachers And Epworth
League Workers By William F. Quillian 1898 The Foote & Davies
Company

12. The Trinity
By Doug Batchelor 2010 Amazing Facts, Inc.

13. An Inquiry Into The Integrity Of The Greek Vulgate, Or Received Text
Of The New Testament By Frederick Nolan 1815 By R. & R, Gilbert

14. Our Authorized Bible Vindicated
By Benjamin G. Wilkinson 2005 Teach Services, Inc.

15. The Revision Revised. Three Articles Reprinted From The 'Quarterly
Review. I. The New Greek Text. II. The New English Version. III.
Westcott And Hort's New Textual Theory. To Which Is Added A
Reply To Bishop Ellicott's Pamphlet In Defence Of The Revisers And
Their Greek Text Of The New Testament: Including A Vindication Of
The Traditional Reading Of 1 Timothy III. 16. By John William
Burgon 1883. John Murry, Albemarle Street.

16. The Identity Of The New Testament Text
By Wilbur N. Pickering 1977 Thomas Nelson Inc., Publishers

17. The Traditional Text Of The Holy Gospels Vindicated And Established
By John William Burgon Edited By Edward Miller 1896 George Bell
And Sons

18. When The KJV Departs From The "Majority" Text
By J.A. Moorman 2010 Bible For Today

19. The Christian Workers' Manual
By H. S. Miller 1922 George H. Doran Company

20. Jesus The True Messiah. A Sermon Delivered In The Jews' Chapel,
Church-Street, Spitalfields, On The Lord's Day Evening, November 19,
1809. By Andrew Fuller. Third Edition. 1810. London: Printed For The
London Society For Promoting Christianity Amongst The Jews, At
Their Office, 6, Devonshire Street, Bishopagate, By B. R. Goakman.
Sold By Black, Parry, And Kingsbury, Leadenhall Street: Conder,
Bucklersbury; Hatchard, Piccadilly; Button. Paternoster Row; And
Seeley, No. 169, Fleet Street.

21. The Conditionalist Faith of Our Fathers (Volume 1 and Volume 2)
By Le Roy Edwin Froom 1966 Review and Herald Publishing
Association

22. The Prophetic Faith of Our Fathers (4 Volumes)
By Le Roy Edwin Froom 1946 Review And Herald Publishing
Association

23. The Fire That Consumes
By Edward Fudge 1982 Providential Press

24. Search For The Immortal Soul
By Daniel Knauft 2006 Torchlight Intel

25. Here And Hereafter or Man in Life and Death The Reward Of The
Righteous And The Destiny Of The Wicked By Uriah Smith 1897
Review and Herald Publishing Assn.

26. Bible Texts Topically Arranged
Compiled By Maude A. Richardson

27. The Great Controversy Between Christ And Satan
By E.G. White Publisher Harvestime Books

28. Bible Readings For The Home
By Unknown Publisher Harvestime Books

29. Answers To Objections
By Francis D. Nichol 1952 Review And Herald Publishing Association

30. Bible Doctrines Containing 150 Lessons, On Creation, Government Of God, Rebellion In Heaven, Fall Of Man, Redemption, Prophecies, Millen-nium, End Of Sinners And Satan, Etc., Etc. By O. A. Johnson 1917 Press of Walla Walla College. Collage Place, Wash.

31. Principles Of Life From The Word Of God
By Unknown 1952 Pacific Press Publishing Association

32. Evidence Of The Truth Of The Christian Religion Derived From The Literal Fulfilment Of Prophecy By Alexander Keith 1839 Harper & Brothers

33. What Are We To Believe? Or, The Testimony Of Fulfilled Prophecy. By John Urquhart 1888 Fleming H. Revell

34. Dissertations On The Prophecies, Which Have Remarkably Been Fulfilled And At This Time Are Fulfilling In The World. By Thomas Newton 1826 London: Printed For B. Blake, Bell Yard, Temple-Bar. (Fourteenth Edition: Complete In One Volume.)

35. The Signs Of The Times, As Denoted By The Fulfillment Of Historical Predictions, Traced Down From The Babylonish Captivity To The Present Time. Vol. I and II By Alexander Keith 1832 Edinburgh: William Whyte & Co.

36. Fulfilled Prophecy A Proof Of The Truth Of Revealed Religion: Being The Warburtonian Lectures For 1854-1858 With An Appendix Of Notes, Including A Full Investigation Of Daniel's Prophecy Of The Seventy Weeks By W. Goode, 1863. London: Hatchard And Co., 187, Piccadilly.

37. Answers To Difficult Bible Texts
By Joe Crews 2013 Amazing Facts, Inc.

38. Daniel And The Revelation: The Response Of History To The Voice Of Prophecy By Uriah Smith 1897 Review & Herald Publishing Assn.

39. The Sure Word Of Prophecy, Shewing The Principle Prophecies Of The Old Testament, Referring Especially To Our Savior, With There Fulfilments In The Gospels, Arranged In The Order Of A Daily Text Book, And Accompanied By Selected Pieces Of Sacred Poetry. By Unknown 1849 Houlston And Stoneman,

40. Facts For The Times. A Collection Of Valuable Historical Extracts On
    A Great Varity Of Subjects, Of Special Interest To The Bible Student,
    From Eminent Authors, Ancient And Modern 1885 Revised By G. I.
    Butler. Review And Herald,

41. Scripture References; Designed For The Use Of Parents, Teachers, And
    Private Christians. By Thomas Chalmers 1817 Printed for John Smith
    And Sons, Glasgow; William Whyte, And Oliphant, Waugh, & Innes,
    Edinburgh; Longman, Hurst, Rees, Orme, & Brown, Ogles, Duncan, &
    Cochran, And Tomas Hamilton, London.

42. Scripture References; Designed For The Use Of Parents, Sabbath
    School Teachers, And Private Christians. By Thomas Chalmers 1825
    Glasgow: Printed For Chalmers & Collins; WM. Whyte & Co. And
    WM. Oliphant, Edinburgh; R. M. Tims, And W. Curry, Jun. & Co.
    Dublin; And G. B. Whittaker, F. Westley, And J. Nisbet, London.

43. Our Day In The Light Of Prophecy
    By W. A. Spicer 1918 Review And Herald Publishing Association

44. The State Of The Dead And The Destiny Of The Wicked.
    By Uriah Smith 1873 Steam Press Of The Seventh-Day Adventist
    Publishing Association, Battle Creek, Mich.:

45. A Supplement To The Authorized English Version Of The New
    Testament By Frederick Henry Scrivener 1845 London William
    Pickering (Volume 1)

46. The Syriac New Testament Translated Into English From The Peshitto
    Version By James Murdock 1915 Boston: H. L. Hastings & Sons

47. In Defense Of The Faith
    By William Henry Branson 1933 Review And Herald

48. The Canon Of The Old And New Testament Ascertained ; Or, The
    Bible Complete Without The Apocrypha & Unwritten Traditions. By
    Archibald Alexander 1826 Princeton Press: Printed And Published By
    D. A. Borrenstein, For G. And C. Carvill, New York.

49. Last-Day Delusions
    By Allen Walker 1957 Southern Publishing Association

50. Romanism And The Reformation: From The Standpoint Of Prophecy.

By H. Grattan Guinness 1887 Hodder And Stoughton

51. Popery Unmasked; Being Thirty Conversations Between Mr. Daylight &
Mr. Twilight, In Which The Peculiar Doctrines, Morals, Government,
And Usages Of The Romish Church Are Truthfully Stated From Her
Own Duly Authorised Works, And Impartially Tried By God's Word,
The Only Unerring Rule Of Doctrine And Duty. By Henry Woodcock
1862 London: Published By Richard Davies, Conference Offices,
Sutton-Street, Commercial-Road, May Be Had Of Primitive Methodist
Ministers,

52. The Works Of Nathaniel Lardner, D.D. In Eleven Volumes: Containing
The Credibility Of The Gospel History; Jewish And Heathen
Testimonies; History Of Heretics; And His Sermons And Tracts: With
General Chronological Tables And Copious Indexes. To The First
Volume Is Prefixed The Life Of The Author, By Andrew Kippis. 1788.
Volume VI. London: Printed For J. Johnson, N 72, St. Paul's Church
Yard.

53. God Cares, Volume 1: The Massage of Daniel for You and Your Family
By Mervyn Maxwell 1981 Pacific Press Publishing Association

54. Salvation: The Way Made Plain.
By James H. Brookes 1884 London: Hodder And Stoughton, 27,
Paternoster Row, MDCCCLXXXIV.

55. Catechetical Lessons On The Ten Commandments. Designed To Aid
The Clergy In Public Catechising. London, John Henry Parker, 377,
Strand; And Broad-Street, Oxford. (1849)

56. The Chronology Of Ezra 7
By S. H. Horn And L. H. Wood 1953 Washington, D.C.: Review And
Herald

57. Testimonies Of Heathen And Christian Writers, Of The First Two
Centuries, To The Truth And Power Of The Gospel. Compiled From
Various Sources, With Notes And Illustrations, &c. By The Thomas
Browne, 1837. London: Printed For J. G. & F. Rivington, St. Paul's
Church Yard, And Waterloo Place, Pall Mall.

58. The Biblical Institute: A Synopsis Of The Lectures On The Principle
Doctrines Of Seventh-Day Adventists Unknown 1878. Oakland, Cal.:
Steam Press Of The Pacific S. D. A. Publishing House.

59. Prophetic Expositions; Or A Connected View Of The Testimony Of The Prophets Concerning The Kingdom Of God And The Time Of Its Establishment. By Josiah Litch. 1842 In Two Volumes Vol. I. Boston: Published By Joshua V. Himes, 14 Devonshire Street.

60. The Canon Of The New Testament Vindicated; In Answer To The Objections Of J. Toland, In His Amyntor. By John Richardson 1619 London: Printed By W. Bowyer, For Richard Sare, Near Gray's-Inn-Gate In Holborn.

61. The Light Of Prophecy Let In On The Dark Places Of The Papacy: Being An Exposition Of 2D Thessal. II. 3-12 Showing Its Exact Fulfilment In The Church Of Rome, With Special Reference To The Aspect Of That Church In The Present Day. By Alexander Hislop, 1846 Edinburgh: William Whyte And Co., Booksellers To The Queen Dowager. Arbroath: P. Wilson; S. Gellatly; And J. Adam. London: Longman And Co. Dublin: W. Curry, Jun. And Co.

62. First Elements Of Sacred Prophecy: Including An Examination Of Several Recent Expositions, And Of The Year-Day Theory. By T. R. Birks, 1843 London: William Edwards Painter, 342, Strand.

63. Evidences Of The Authenticity, Inspiration And Canonical Authority Of The Holy Scriptures. By Archibald Alexander 1836 Presbyterian Board Of Publication And Sabbath-School Work.

64. The Approaching End Of The Age Viewed In The Light Of History, Prophecy, And Science. By H. Grattan Guinness 1878 London Hodder And Stoughton, 27, Paternoster Row.

65. The New Testament Of Our Lord And Saviour Jesus Christ: Published In 1526. Being The First Translation From The Greek Into English, By That Eminent Scholar And Martyr, William Tyndale. Reprinted Verbatim : With A Memoir Of His Life And Writings, By George Offor. Together With The Proceedings And Correspondence Of Henry VIII., Sir T. More, And Lord Cromwell. 1836. London : Samuel Bagster, 15, Paternoster Row : At The Warehouse For Bibles, New Testaments, Prayer Books, Psalters, And Concordances, In Ancient And Modern Languages.

66. The New Testament Of Our Lord And Saviour Jesus Christ. By William Tyndale, The Martyr. The Original Edition, 1526, Being The First

Vernacular Translation From The Greek. With A Memoir Of His Life And Writings. To Which Are Annexed, The Essential Variations Of Coverdale's, Thomas Matthew's, Cranmer's, The Genevn, And The Bishops' Bibles, As Marginal Readings. By J. P. Dabney. 1837. Andover: Printed And Published By Gould & Newman; From The London Edition Of Bagster. New York: Corner Of Fulton And Nassac Streets.

67. Observations Upon The Prophecies Of Daniel, And The Apocalypse Of St. John. In Two Parts By Isaac Newton. 1733. London: Printed By J. Darby And T. Browne In Bartholomew-Close.

68. The Commandment To Restore And Build Jerusalem.
By J. N. Andrews 1865. Steam Press Of The Seventh-Day Adventist Publishing Association, Battle Creek, Mich.

69. The Sanctuary And The Twenty – Three Hundred Days Of Daniel VIII. 14. By Uriah Smith 1877. Steam Press Of The Seventh-Day Adventist Publishing Association Battle Creek, Mich.

70. The Good News Of Daniel 8:14
By Daniel E. Augsburger 1981, 2003 Teach Services, Inc.

71. Daniel The Seer Of Babylon
By Gerhard Pfandl 2004 Review And Herald Publishing Association

72. Synopsis Of The Present Truth: A Brief Exposition Of The Views Of S. D. Adventists. By Uriah Smith 1884 Battle Creek, Mich. : Seventh-Day Adventist Publishing Association. Pacific Press, Oakland, Cal. The Present Truth, Great Grimsby, Eng. Les Signes Des Temps, Bale, Suisse. Tidernes Tegn, Christiana, Norway.

73. A Collection Of The Promises Of Scripture, Under Their Proper Heads. In Two Parts. Representing I. The Blessings Promised. And, II. The Duties To Which Promises Are Made. With An Appendix, Relating To The Future State Of The Church. And An Introduction, Containing Observations Upon The Exclllency And Use Of The Promises, And Directions For The Right Application Of Them. By Samuel Clark 1805, Edinburgh: Printed By Thomas Turnbull, Canongate, For Denham & Dick, 19, Collegestreet, W. Baynes, Paternoster-Row ; Williams & Smith, Stationers' Court ; And R. Ogle, Great Turnstile, London.

74. The Canon Of The Holy Scriptures From The Double Point Of View

Of Science And Of Faith. By L. Gaussen 1862 London: James Nisbet And Co., 21 Berners Street

75. An Introduction To The Critical Study And Knowledge Of The Holy Scriptures By Thomas Hartwell Horne 1825 From The Fourth Corrected Edition. Illustrated With Numerous Maps And Fac-Similes Of Biblical Manuscripts. Volume II. Philadelphia: Published By E. Littell. Sold Also By G. & C. Carvill, New-York; And Cummings, Hilliard, & Co.Boston.

76. A Scholastical History Of The Canon Of The Holy Scriptures; Or The Certain And Indubitate Books Thereof, As They Are Received In The Church Of England: Compiled By Dr. Cosin 1683 London, Printed By E. Tyler And R. Holt For Robert Pawlett, At The Sign Of The Bible In Chancery-Lane, Near Fleet-Street.

77. The Coptic Version Of The New Testament In The Northern Dialect Otherwise Called Memphitic And Bohairic With Introduction, Critical Apparatus, And Literal English Translation Volume II The Gospels Of S. Luke And S. John Edited From MS. Huntington 17 In The Bodleian Library 1898 Oxford At The Clarendon Press (Four Volume Set)

78. The Coptic Version Of The New Testament In The Southern Dialect Otherwise Called Sahidic And Thebaic With Critical Apparatus, Literal English Translation And Register And Notes Of Fragments Volume VI The Acts Of The Apostles 1922 Oxford At The Clarendon Press

79. A Dictionary Of The Bible By John D. Davis 1898 Philadelphia The Westminster Press

80. Studying Together A Ready-reference Bible Handbook By Mark Finley 1995 Hart Research Center (Revised Edition)

81. The Englishman's Hebrew And Chaldee Concordance Of The Old Testament Being An Attempt At A Verbal Connexion Between The Original And The English Translation With Indexes A List Of Proper Names And Their Occurrences ECT. Vol. I. By George V. Wigram 1843 London: Longman, Green, Brown, And Longmans, Paternoster Row.

82. The Englishman's Greek Concordance Of The New Testament: Being An Attempt At A Verbal Connection Between The Greek And The English Texts; Including A Concordance To The Proper Names; With

Indexes, Greek-English And English-Greek. By George V. Wigram 1870 London: Samuel Bagster And Sons, 15, Paternoster Row.

83. A Hebrew And English Lexicon Of The Old Testament With An Appendix Containing The Biblical Aramaic Based On The Lexicon Of William Gesenius As Translated By Edward Robinson By Francis Brown With The co-operation of S. R. Driver and Charles A. Briggs 1906 Oxford At The Clarendon Press

84. A Greek-English Lexicon Of The New Testament Being Grimm's Wilke's Clavis (Clavis or is it Tlavis) Novi Testamenti (Testameuti) Translated Revised And Enlarged By Joseph Henry Thayer 1892 Edinburgh T. & T. Clark, 38 George Street 1892

85. The Bible Of Every Land. A History Of The Sacred Scriptures In Every Language And Dialect Into Which Translations Have Been Made: Illustrated By Specimen Portions In Native Characters; Series Of Alphabets ; Coloured Ethnographical Maps, Tables, Indexes, ECT. New Edition, Enlarged And Enriched. London: Samuel Bagster And Sons : At The Warehouse For Bibles, New Testaments, Church Services, Prayer Books, Lexicons, Grammars, Concordances, And Psalters, In Ancient And Modern Languages ; 15, Paternoster Row. 1860.

86. The Bible In Manny Tongues.
London: The Religious Tract Society ; Instituted 1799.

87. CYCLOPÆDIA Of Biblical, Theological, And Ecclesiastical Literature. Prepared By John M'Clintock And James Strong 1894 New York: Harper & Brothers, Publishers, Franklin Square Vol. II.-C, D

88. A Short Account Of The Lives And Martyrdom Of The Apostles, Evangelists, Disciples, And Earliest Fathers Of The Church, Who Suffered For The Truth Of Christianity. Compiled From Holy Scripture, And Ancient Church History, By Louisa Charlotte Frampton. 1860 London: Rivingtons, Waterloo Place.

89. Past, Present, And Future
By James Edson White 1914 Southern Publishing Association

90. Our Banquet: He Brought Me To The Banqueting House And His Banner Over Me Was Love By H. A. ST. John. 1894

91. Historical Evidence Of The New Testament. An Inductive Study In

Christian Evidences. The Facts Mentioned In The New Testament Demonstrated To Be Historical By The Worst Enemies Of Christianity Who Lived In The First Three Centuries Of Our Era, Confirmed By As Many Christian Writers Of Fame, Contemporaries Who Wrote In Different Countries And Periods: The Whole Reconfirmed By Many Remarkable Evidences Recently Discovered: Ancient Documents, Monuments, Arches, Inscriptions, Coins, Superscriptions, And Christian Art. By S. L. Bowman 1903 Cincinnati: Jennings And Pye. New York: Eaton And Mains.

92. The Evidences of Christianity By W. Paley 1837. London: T. Allman, 42, Holborn Hill

93. Biblical Antiquities By John Jahn Translated From The Latin, With Additions And Corrections By Thomas C. Upham 1832 London: Thomas Ward And Co, Paternoster Row.

94. Essay On The Right Estimation Of Manuscript Evidence In The Text Of The New Testament. By Thomas Rawson Birks 1878 London: Macmillan And Co.

95. Drama Of The Ages By William Henry Branson 1950 Review And Herald Publishing Association / Southern Publishing Association

96. Doctrinal Discussions A Compilation Of Articles Originally Appearing In The Ministry, June, 1960- July, 1961, In Answer To Walter R. Martin's Book The Truth About Seventh-day Adventism. Date Unknown. Prepared By The Ministerial Association General Conference Of Seventh-day Adventists Washington 12, D.C. Review And Herald Publishing Association.

97. The Law And The Sabbath By Allen Walker 1953 Southern Publishing Association

98. Our Changing World Whither Bound? By Alonzo L. Baker, Roy F. Cottrell, Carlyle B. Haynes, Gwynne Dalrymple, Frederick Lee, Francis D. Nichol, Robert B. Thurber 1933 Southern Publishing Association / Pacific Press Publishing Association

99. Seventh-day Adventist Bible Dictionary Complete With Atlas By Siegfried H. Horn 1960 Review And Herald

100. New Age Bible Versions By G. A. Riplinger 1993 A. V. Publications

Corporation

101. Questions And Answers Gathered From The Question Corner Department Of The Signs Of The Times By Milton C. Wilcox 1911 Pacific Press Publishing Association

102. The Return Of Jesus. An Earnest Review Of The Scriptural Evidences Which Establish The Great Christian Doctrine Of The Second Coming Of Christ, Together With A Close Study Of The Prophecies Relating To This Glorious Event And Fulfilment Of These Prophecies In The Present Generation. By Carlyle B. Haynes 1917 Southern Publishing Association

103. The Two Laws, As Set Forth In The Scriptures Of The Old And New Testaments. By D. M. Canright. 1882. Battle Creek Mich.: Seventh-Day Adventist Publishing Association.

104. Which Version? Authorized Or Revised? By Philip Mauro. Date Unknown. Scripture Truth Depot.

105. The Way Made Plain By James H. Brookes 1816 Philadelphia: American Sunday-School Union, 1816 Chestnut Street

106. The Divine Programme Of The World's History. By Mr. And Mrs. H. Grattan Guinness 1888 London: Hodder And Stoughton, 27, Paternoster Row.

107. The Four Prophetic Empires, And The Kingdom Of Messiah: Being An Exposition Of The First Two Visions Of Daniel. By T. R. Birks 1845. Seeley, Burnside, And Seeley, Fleet Street, London.

108. Dissertations On The Genuineness Of Daniel And The Integrity Of Zechariah. By E. W. Hengstenberg, Translated By B. P. Pratten. 1848. Edinburgh: T. & T. Clark, 38. George Street; London: Seeley & Co. ; Ward & Co. ; Jackson & Walford, &c, Dublin: John Robertson. –New York : Wiley & Putnam. –Boston Crocker & Brewster. –Philadelphia : J. W. Moore.

109. Daniel The Prophet. Nine Lectures, Delivered In The Divinity School Of The University Of Oxford, With Copious Notes. By E. B. Pusey, 1864. Sold By John Henry And James Parker, Oxford, And 337, Strand, London; Rivingtons, Waterloo Place, London, And 41, High Street, Oxford,

110. A Commentary On The Book Of Daniel. By Moses Stuart. 1850. Boston: Published By Crocker & Brewster.

111: Prophetic Lights: Some Of The Prominent Prophecies Of The Old And New Testament Interpreted By The Bible And History. By E. J. Waggoner. 1888. Pacific Press Publishing Company.

112. Critical History And Defence Of The Old Testament Canon. By Moses Stuart, Edited By Peter Lorimer, 1849 London: William Tegg And Co., Cheapside.

113. Did Daniel Write Daniel? The Genuineness And Authenticity Of The Book Of Daniel Discussed. By Joseph D. Wilson. Date Unknown. Charles C. Cook 150 Nassau Street New York, N. Y.

114. Our Paradise Home The Earth Made New And The Restoration Of All Things. By S. H. Lane. 1903. Review And Herald Publishing Association

115. Two Beasts, Three Deadly Wounds, And Fourteen Popes. By Russell R. Standish And Colin D. Standish 2001 Hartland Publications

116. Horæ Apocalypticæ ; Or, A Commentary On The Apocalypse, Critical And Historical; Including Also An Examination Of The Chief Prophecies Of Daniel. Illustrated By An Apocalyptic Chart, And Engravings From Medals And Other Extant Monuments Of Antiquity. By E. B. Elliott. 1847. Seeley, Burnside, And Seeley; Fleet Street, London. Vol. III.

117. The Four Gospels, As Interpreted By The Early Church: A Commentary On The Authorized English Version Of The Gospel According To S. Matthew, S. Mark, S. Luke, & S. John, Compared With The Sinaitic, The Vatican, And Alexandrian MSS., And Also With The Vulgate. By Francis Henry Dunwell. 1876. London: Printed By William Clowes & Sons, Stamford Street And Charing Cross.

118. A Guide To The Textual Criticism Of The New Testament. By Edward Miller. 1886. George Bell And Sons, York Street, Covent Garden, London.

119. The Canon Of The Holy Scriptures Examined In The Light Of History. By L. Gaussen Translated From The French, And Abridged

By Edward N. Kirk. 1862. American Tract Society, Boston.

120. A Dissertation On The Rule Of Faith; Delivered At Cincinnati, Ohio, At The Annual Meeting Of The American Bible Society, And Published At Their Request. By Gardiner Spring. 1844. New York: Leavitt, Trow, & Co., 194 Broadway.

121. The Bible Not Of Man: Or, The Argument For The Divine Origin Of The Sacred Scriptures. Drawn From The Scriptures Themselves. By Gardiner Spring. 1847. Published By The American Tract Society. 150 Nassau-Street, New-York.

122. A Disputation On Holy Scripture, Against The Papists, Especially Bellarmine And Stapleton. By William Whitaker. Translated And Edited For The Parker Society By William Fitzgerald 1849. Cambridge: Printed At The University Press.

123. Fathers, Popes, & Councils, And Eminent Roman Catholic Writers; Together With Other Authorities Of That Persuasion; In Favor Of The Reading Of The Holy Scriptures, By All Manner Of Persons. (Note: Compiler/Author, Date, Publisher, All Unknown)

124. Our Brief Against Rome By Charles Stuteville Isaacson 1905 London The Religious Tract Society

125. Facts And Assertions: Or A Brief And Plain Exhibition Of The Incongruity Of The Peculiar Doctrines Of The Church Of Rome With Those, Both Of The Sacred Scriptures, And Of The Early Writers Of The Christian Church Catholic. By George Stanley Faber 1831. London: Printed For C. J. G. & F. Rivington, Booksellers to the Society for Promoting Christian Knowledge, St. Paul's Church-Yard, And Waterloo-Place, Pall-Mall.

126. Delineation Of Roman Catholicism, Drawn From The Authentic And Acknowledged Standards Of The Church Of Rome: Namely, Her Creeds, Catechisms, Decisions Of Councils, Papal Bulls, Roman Catholic Writers, The Records Of History, Ect. Ect.: In Which The Peculiar Doctrines, Morals, Government, And Usages Of The Church Of Rome, Are Stated, Treated At Large, And Confuted. By Charles Elliott 1841 New-York: Published By George Lain, For The Methodist Episcopal Church, At The Conference Office, 200 Mulberry-Street. J. Collord, Printer. Volume I

127. The Church Of Rome Examined: Or, Can I Ever Enter The Church Of Rome, So Long As I Believe The Whole Bible? A Question Submitted To The Conscience Of Every Christian Reader. Translated From The French Of The C. Malan. By The John Cormack, 1840. London: James Nisbet And Co. Berners S J. Johnstone, Edinburgh ; William Collins, Glasgow ; W. Curry, & Co. Dublin ; And M'Come, Belfast.

128. A Plain Protestant Manuel, Or, Certain Plain Sermons On The Scriptures, The Church, And The Sacraments, &c. &c. &c. In Which The Corruptions Of The Romish Church Are Evidently Set Forth. By John Wood Warter 1851. London: Francis & John Rivington, St. Paul's Church Yard, And Waterloo Place.

129. Papal Error; Their Rise And Progress. By Unknown. London: The Religious Tract Society; Instituted 1799. Sold At The Depository, 56, Paternoster Row, And 65, St. Paul's Churchyard; And By The Booksellers.

130. A Protestant's Appeal To The Douay Bible, And Other Roman Catholic Standards, In Support Of The Doctrines Of The Reformation. By John Jenkins. 1853. Fourth Edition. Montreal: Wesleyan Book Depot, Great St. James Street.

131. Doctrinal Treaties And Introduction To Different Portions Of The Holy Scriptures By William Tyndale, Martyr, 1536. Edited For The Parker Society By Henry Walter 1848. Cambridge: Printed At The University Press.

132. The Apostasy Of The Church Of Rome, And The Identity Of The Papal Power, With The Man Of Sin And Son Of Perdition Of St. Paul's Prophecy, In The Second Epistle To The Thessalonians, Proved From The Testimony Of Scripture And History. By William Cuninghame. 1818. Glasgow: Printed By Young, Gallie, & Co.

133. Christ And Antichrist Or Jesus Of Nazareth Proved To Be The Messiah And The Papacy Proved To Be The Antichrist Predicted In The Holy Scriptures. By Samuel J. Cassels. 1846. Philadelphia: Presbyterian Board Of Publication.

134. Truth Triumphant The Church In The Wilderness By B. G. Wilkinson 2005 Teach Services Inc.

135. Looking Unto Jesus: A View Of The Everlasting Gospel; Or, The Soul's Eying Of Jesus, As Carrying On The Great Work Of Man's Salvation, From First To Last. By Isaac Ambrose. 1832. Pittsburg: Published By Luke Loomis & Co.

136. The Story Of Daniel The Prophet By Stephen N. Haskell 1908. Bible Training School South Lancaster, Mass.

137. Why Johnny Can't Read By Rudolf Flesch 1955 Harper & Row, Publishers

138. Why Johnny Still Can't Read By Rudolf Flesch 1981 HarperCollins

139. The Ten Commandments Twice Removed By Danny Shelton And Shelley Quinn 2004 Remnant Publications, Inc.

140. History Of The Sabbath And The First Day Of The Week. By J. N. Andrews And L. R. Conradi 1912 Review & Herald Publishing Association

141. The Christian Sabbath Is It Saturday Or Sunday? A Careful Study Of This Important Religious Question From The Standpoint Of The Scriptures Of Truth. By Carlyle B. Haynes

142. Notes. Critical, Illustrative, And Practical, On The Book Of Daniel, With An Introductory Dissertation. By Albert Barns 1853. New-York: Leavitt & Allen, 27 Dey-Street.

143. The Great Empires Of Prophecy From Babylon To The Fall Of Rome By Alonzo Trevier Jones 1898 Review And Herald Publishing Company

144. Questions And Answers Volume II Gathered From The Question Department Of The Signs Of The Times By Milton C. Wilcox 1919 Pacific Press Publishing Association

145. Maranatha – The Lord Is Coming By Ellen G. White 1976 Review And Herald Publishing Association

146. The Atoning Work Of Christ His Sacrifice And Priestly Ministry By C. H. Watson 1934 Review And Herald Publishing Association

147. The Second Coming Of Christ, Or, A Brief Exposition Of Matthew

Twenty-Four By James White 1873 Steam Press Of The Seventh-Day Adventist Publishing House

148. Collection Of Facts For The Times, Consisting Of Valuable Extracts From Eminent Authors By Unknown 1875 Steam Press Of The Seventh-Day Adventist Publishing Association, Battle Creek, Mich. (Second Edition, Revised.)

149. The Pilgrim's Progress From This World To That Which Is To Come; Delivered Under The Similitude Of A Dream. By John Bunyan. To Which Is Added A Life Of Bunyan, By Himself; Or, Grace Abounding To The Chief Of Sinners. 1859. By John Bunyan. Philadelphia: J. W. Bradley, 48 North Fourth St.

150. Fox's Book Of Martyrs, Or A History Of The Lives, Sufferings, And Triumphant Deaths Of The Primitive Protestant Martyrs, From The Introduction Of Christianity To The Latest Periods Of Pagan, Popish, And Infidel Persecution. Embracing, Together With The Usual Subjects Contained In Similar Works, The Recent Persecutions In The Cantons Of Switzerland, The Perse-cutions Of The Methodists And Baptist Missinaries In The West India Islands; And The Narrative Of The Conversion, Capture, Long Imprisonment, And Cruel Sufferings Of Asaad Shidiar, A Native Palestine. Likewise A Sketch Of The French Revolution, As Connected With Persecution. Compiled From Fox's Book Of Martyrs, And Other Authentic Sources. 1881. Philadelphia: E. Claxton & Company, 930 Market Street.

151. The Table Talk Or, Familiar Discourse Of Martin Luther. Translated By William Hazlitt. 1848. London: David Bogue, Fleet Street.

152. Our Times And Their Meaning
By Carlyle B. Haynes 1929 Southern Publishing Association

153. The History Of Romanism: From The Earliest Corruptions Of Christianity To The Present Time. With Full Chronological Table, Analytical And Alphabetical Indexes And Glossary. Illustrated By Numerous Accurate And Highly Finished Engravings Of Its Ceremonies, Superstitions, Persecutions, And Historical Incidents. By John Dowling 1845 New York: Edward Walker, 114 Fulton Street.

154. History Of The Reformation In The Sixteenth Century.
By J. H. Merle D'Aubigne 1846 Blackie And Son: Queen Street, Glasgow; South College Street Edinburgh; And Warwick Square

London. (In Three Volumes)

155. The True Nature Of Imposture Fully Displayed In The Life Of
Mahomet. With A Discourse Annexed, For The Vindication Of
Christianity From This Charge; Offered To The Consideration Of The
Deists Of The Present Age. By Humphrey Prideaux 1697 London:
Printed For William Rogers; At The Sun Against St. Dunstan's
Church, In Fleetstreet. M DC XC VII .

156. Assault On The Remnant
By Ted Schultz 2012 Dog Ear Publishing

157. The Evidences Of Christianity In Their External Or Historical
Division: Exhibited In A Course Of Lectures, By Charles Pettit
M'ilvaine 1832 Published By The American Tract Society, 150 Nassau-
Street, New York.

158. Divine Revelation; Its Evidences, External, Internal, And Collateral.
Together With Its Canonical Authority And Plenary Inspiration. By
Daniel Dewar 1854 London: Houlston And Stoneman, 65, Paternoster
Row.

159. The Septuagint Version Of The Old Testament, With An English
Translation: And With Various Readings And Critical Notes. 1884
London: Samuel Bagster And Sons, Limited, 15, Paternoster Row.

160. The Gothic And Anglo-Saxon Gospels In Parallel Columns With The
Versions Of Wycliffe And Tyndale; Arranged, With Preface And
Notes, By Joseph Bosworth Assisted By George Waring 1888.
London: Reeves & Turner, 196 Strand.

161. The Gospel According To S. John, Translated From The Eleven
Oldest Versions Except The Latin, And Compared With The English
Bible; With Notes On Every One Of The Alterations Proposed By
The Five Clergymen In Their Revised Version Of This Gospel,
Published In MDCCCLVII. By S. C. Malan 1862 London: Joseph
Masters, Aldersgate Street, And New Bond Street. MDCCCLXII.

162. The Holy Bible, Containing The Olde Testament, And The New.
Newly Tranflated Out Of The Originall Tongnes: And With The
Former Tranflations Diligently Compared And Reuifed, By His
Maiefties fpeciall Commandeincut. Anno 1617. Imprinted At London
By Robert Barker,. Printer To The Kings Moft Excellent Matcftte.

(Note: The "f" are "s")

163. The Holy Bible, Containing The Old And New Covenants, Literally
     And Idiomatically Translated Out Of The Original Languages. By
     Robert Young 1863 Edinburgh, Dublin, & London ; A. Fullarton &
     Company.

164. The New Testament Octapla: Eight English Versions of the New
     Testament By Luther A. Weigle 1946 Thomas Nelson & Sons

165. The English Hexapla: Exhibiting the Six Important English
     Translations of the New Testament Scriptures ; the Original Greek
     Text after Scholz Publisher London : Samuel Bagster and Sons 1841

166. The Bible-Reading Gazette
     By Numerous Authors 1888 Review and Herald

167. Bible Readings For The Home Circle
     By Unknown 1888 Review and Herald Publishing Company

168. Bible Readings For The Home Circle
     By Unknown 1888 Review and Herald Publishing House,

Bible Studies as Found in The Back of the Respective Bibles :

169. The Search For Certainty
     By Mark Finley Date Unknown It Is Written : This Bible Study Found
     in the back of a King James Version of The Holy Bible. It Is Written
     Study Edition. Seminars Unlimited Edition

170. H.M.S. Richards Bible Subject Helps
     By H.M.S. Richards 1966 : This Bible Study Found in the back of a
     King James Version of The Holy Bible. Brown & Marley

Books By Joshua Alan Fogle

171. Lost Truth About God
     By Joshua A. Fogle 2015 CreateSpace Independent Publishing Platform
     First Edition June 18, 2015

172. The 40 Day Devotional Journey Through The Bible
     By Joshua A. Fogle 2015 CreateSpace Independent Publishing Platform

First Edition August 23, 2015

173. The Deity Of Christ Defended
    By Joshua A. Fogle 2017 CreateSpace Independent Publishing Platform
    First Edition October 15, 2017

174. Lost Truth About Bible Prophecy
    By Joshua A. Fogle 2017 CreateSpace Independent Publishing Platform
    First Edition October 15, 2017

175. Evidence That Proves Christianity True
    By Joshua A. Fogle 2018 CreateSpace Independent Publishing Platform
    First Edition July 15, 2018

176. The Holy Trinity Defended
    By Joshua A. Fogle 2018 CreateSpace Independent Publishing Platform
    First Edition December 7, 2018

177. What Happens When You Die
    By Joshua A. Fogle 2019 Independently Published
    First Edition July 28, 2019

178. The Forgotten Faith Of Jesus
    By Joshua A. Fogle 2021 Independently Published
    First Edition May 23-24, 2021

179. Evidence That Proves The Existence Of God
    By Joshua A. Fogle 2021 Independently Published
    First Edition May 30-31, 2021

180. The Holy Bible And The Koran Compared
    By Joshua A. Fogle 2021 Independently Published
    First Edition June 2-3, 2021

181. The Holy Trinity Shown To Be Jehovah Our One God
    By Joshua A. Fogle 2021 Independently Published
    First Edition June 14-15, 2021

182. Fulfilled Prophecy Answers The Bible Version Debate
    By Joshua A. Fogle 2021 Independently Published
    First Edition July 12-13, 2021

183. The Bible Question And Answer Devotional

By Joshua A. Fogle 2021 Independently Published
First Edition July 28-29, 2021

184. The Seventy Weeks Prophecy Of Daniel 9:24-27
By Joshua A. Fogle 2021 Independently Published
First Edition November 13(17), 2021

185. Three Major Problems Within The Seventh-Day Adventist Church
By Joshua A. Fogle 2021 Independently Published
First Edition December 3, 2021

186. Roman Catholicism Refuted By The Bible And The Early Christian
Church By Joshua A. Fogle 2022 Independently Published
First Edition January 16-17, 2022

187. The Holy Bible And The Book Of Mormon Compared
By Joshua A. Fogle 2022 Independently Published
First Edition February 20-21. 2022

188. The Basics Of Christianity
By Joshua A. Fogle 2022 Independently Published

Bible Commentaries :

189. Barnes' Notes on the Bible
By Albert Barnes 1834

190. Benson Commentary on the Old and New Testament
By Joseph Benson 1846

191. Clarke's Commentary on the Bible
By Adam Clarke 1831

192. Gill's Exposition on the Entire Bible
By John Gill 1746-63

193. A Commentary, Critical, Practical, and Explanatory on the Old and
New Testament By Robert Jamieson, A. R. Fausset and David Brown
1882

194. Jamieson, Fausset, and Brown's Commentary on the Whole Bible
By Robert Jamieson, A. R. Fausset and David Brown

195. The New Testament Commentary For English Readers
    Edited By C. J. Ellicott 1884

196. An Old Testament Commentary For English Readers
    Edited By Charles John Ellicott 1882

197. Matthew Poole's Commentary

Articles :

198. The 70 Weeks and 457 B.C.
    By Angel Manuel Rodríguez, April 1994 Biblical Research Institute

199. When Did the Seventy Weeks of Daniel 9:24 Begin?
    By William H. Shea 1991 Journal of the Adventist Theological Society

200. Stephen P. Bohr's Notes on Daniel 9
    By Stephen P. Bohr

201. How Should We Address God?
    By Frank B. Holbrook 1998 Biblical Research Institute General
    Conference of Seventh-day Adventists

202. What About The Apocrypha?
    By Ángel Manuel Rodríguez 6/07 Biblical Research Institute
    General Conference of Seventh-day Adventists

203. Is The Bible Trustworthy And Reliable?
    By Ekkehardt Mueller January 2003 Biblical Research Institute
    General Conference of Seventh-day Adventists

204. Stephen P. Bohr's Notes On Daniel 7
    By Stephen P. Bohr

205. Response To: "The Investigative Judgment: A Bible Based Doctrine?"
    By Angel Manuel Rodríguez Nov. 1997 Biblical Research Institute

206. Is Jesus God?
    By Ekkehardt Mueller October 2008 Biblical Research Institute
    General Conference of Seventh-day Adventists

Internet :

207. Amazing Discoveries .Tv
     By Walter Veith and Victor Gill

208. Amazing Facts .Org
     By Joe Crews and Doug Batchelor

209. Hope Channel (hopetv.org)

210. Three Angels Broadcasting Network (3ABN.org)

211. Biblical Research Institute (AdventistBiblicalResearch.org)

212. Signs Of The Times (SignsTimes.com)

213. It Is Written .com

214. Secrets Unsealed .Org
     By Stephen P. Bohr

215. Adventist Archives .Org
     By The Office of Archives, Statistics, and Research (ASTR)

Seek ye the LORD while he may be found, call ye upon him while he is near : (Isaiah 55:6)

Please be Advised that all Bible Readings and Quotes Used in this Book unless otherwise noted or implied are Taken From the King James Version of The Holy Bible.

Disclaimer: All internet/web sites mentioned are used and or visited at your own personal risk the author and publisher make no warranty as to what may occur should you use and or visit any of the internet/web sites mentioned.

All For Christ Or Nothing.

BACK COVER

What are the basics of Christianity? What do Christians believe? What is it that Christian know, that others do not know? What don't I know? What should I know as a Christian? Have you ever thought any of these questions to yourself? Have you ever asked: Who is God? Is God real? What happens to us when we die? As a believer myself, I am sure that there are many Christians and none Christians who haven't the slightest idea what it is that Christianity is all about even it they think they do. For Christianity in the popular media, the mega-churches, political Christianity, liberal Christianity, and conspiracy theory Christianity is far different then what The Bible actually teaches and says. Now rather then having an expose on these things, we are instead going to discuss using The Bible and historical documentation, exactly what Christianity is and is not, for we will see that both The Bible and early Christianity declare that The Holy Bible alone is Christian doctrine in entirety, and incorporated with that, we will see the historical attestation for The Biblical Canon, that is, The Books of The Bible, and a discussion on Bible Versions. Then we will move on to what The Bible actually teaches on how salvation from sin Biblically works, how a Christian is to Biblically live their life, what happens when we die and the hereafter, The Holy Trinity, and the importance and necessity of keeping The Law of God and The Seventh-day Sabbath of God, and what it truly means when Scripture says to not judge others, as well as how faith and works combine in Holy Writ.